Pulpit Apologist

Pulpit Apologist

The Vital Link between Preaching and Apologetics

THOMAS J. GENTRY II

WIPF & STOCK · Eugene, Oregon

PULPIT APOLOGIST
The Vital Link between Preaching and Apologetics

Copyright © 2020 Thomas J. Gentry II. All rights reserved. Except for brief quotations in critical publications or reviews, no part of this book may be reproduced in any manner without prior written permission from the publisher. Write: Permissions, Wipf and Stock Publishers, 199 W. 8th Ave., Suite 3, Eugene, OR 97401.

Wipf & Stock
An Imprint of Wipf and Stock Publishers
199 W. 8th Ave., Suite 3
Eugene, OR 97401

www.wipfandstock.com

PAPERBACK ISBN: 978-1-5326-9504-9
HARDCOVER ISBN: 978-1-5326-9505-6
EBOOK ISBN: 978-1-5326-9506-3

Manufactured in the U.S.A.   01/09/20

For Zachary Scott Bollman
κήρυξον τὸν λόγον ἐπίστηθι εὐκαίρως ἀκαίρως
ἔλεγξον ἐπιτίμησον παρακάλεσον ἐν πάσῃ
μακροθυμίᾳ καὶ διδαχῇ

Contents

Introduction: Preaching and Apologetics? | ix

CHAPTER 1
Helping Seekers Find:
Apologetic Preaching and Evangelism | 1

CHAPTER 2
Helping Believers Grow:
Apologetic Preaching and Discipleship | 13

CHAPTER 3
God is Good:
The Special Relationship between Preaching and Moral Apologetics | 24

CHAPTER 4
A Reasonable Proclamation:
Apologetic Preaching and Making Arguments | 31

CHAPTER 5
Preacher, Try This:
The STEPS Model for Apologetic Preaching | 44

Conclusion: A Plea for Apologetic Preaching | 61

Bibliography | 67
Index | 71

Introduction
Preaching and Apologetics?

Sheila's friend Mary invited her to a special Sunday evening service at her church designed to answer questions about the Christian faith for skeptics and seekers. As a curious non-Christian, Sheila was intrigued by the invitation and decided to attend one of the services. Mary's pastor began each message at these services with a question about Christianity, and the night Sheila attended the question was, "Does God really exist?" As Sheila listened to the message, the pastor explained that each person has an innate sense of what is right and what is wrong, and that this innate sense of morality is a clue to God's existence. Sheila was challenged by the message and, though she did not respond to the brief gospel invitation offered at the end of the service, she did promise to attend again with Mary. The preaching Sheila heard offered answers to questions about God, and she began to seriously consider the claims of Christianity.

Raised in a Christian home, John regularly attended church and other activities, including participating in his youth group and actively sharing his faith in Jesus. Upon graduating high school John enrolled as a commuter student at the local state university and, as part of his course of general studies, took a course in cultural anthropology. His professor was an atheist and an outspoken critic of religion in general, especially Christianity, and soon the professor's challenges led John to wrestle with profound and persistent doubts about the existence of God and the reliability of the

Introduction

Bible. Thus, when John's pastor began a series of sermons on why the Christian worldview makes sense and the Bible can be trusted, John found answers to his doubts, and his faith was strengthened. The preaching John heard helped him find reasons to believe, and he grew as a disciple of Jesus Christ.

What do these examples of preaching have in common?[1] Though the primary purpose of the preaching in Sheila's instance was to make a compelling case for Christianity to skeptics and seekers, and the primary purpose in John's instance was to strengthen a disciple's faith, both messages involved apologetics. However, is this a legitimate role for preaching, whether to those who are already Christians or to seekers and skeptics? Is there a nexus—a central link or connection—between apologetics and preaching for discipleship and evangelism, or are these separate activities?[2] In consideration of these and related questions, I invite you to join me in an investigation into the relationship between apologetics and preaching. In the chapters that follow I explore several important areas in this regard, but first, a bit more about preaching to help set the stage for our exploration.

Preaching in a Post-everything Context

Preaching is a fundamental and regularly occurring expression of a pastor's work within most congregations, both in terms of evangelism and discipleship. Wayne McDill concludes that "of all the tasks to be done in ministry, preaching is surely one of the most

---

1. Though the names in each instance are changed, each of these situations describes my real-life experience with apologetics and preaching. Further, while discussed separately in another chapter, discipleship and evangelism could occur in either of the preaching examples provided. A message may be primarily designed for discipleship, but it is certainly possible and likely that evangelistic implications follow, and vice versa. However, as considered in chapter 3, effective apologetic preaching generally has a specific audience in mind—sometimes disciples and sometimes seekers and skeptics.

2. Nexus comes from the from the Latin *nectere*, meaning to bind or tie. Vocabulary.com Dictionary, "nexus," https://www.vocabulary.com/dictionary/nexus.

important."[3] Paul the apostle admonished his young protégé, Timothy, who was also a pastor and mentor to other pastors, to "give attention to . . . exhortation" (1 Tim 4:13), to "Preach the word! Be ready in season and out of season. Convince, rebuke, exhort, with all longsuffering and teaching" (2 Tim 4:2), and to "do the work of an evangelist" (2 Tim 4:5).[4] In these directives to Timothy, Paul describes the centrality of the pastor's role as preacher—to exhort, teach, and evangelize. Haddon Robinson explains that the pastor's call to preaching is so significant because "through the preaching of the Scriptures, God encounters men and women to bring them to salvation . . . and to richness and ripeness of Christian character."[5] Though there may be exceptions to the centrality of preaching in a pastor's ministry, such as instances of multi-pastor churches where one pastor focuses on counseling and another on student ministries and so on, the general expectation of lead pastors is that they will preach.

However, amid the prevailing post-modern and post-Christian milieu in much of the world, the audience to which the pastor delivers his message is increasingly ignorant of and unsure of the veracity of even its most basic elements. According to James White, 23 percent of adults in the United States consider themselves as having no religious affiliation, and nearly 19 percent of adults claim to be former Christians.[6] Add to these statistics the widespread veneration of philosophical and religious pluralism, and one begins to recognize the challenge today's pastor faces when standing behind the pulpit and proclaiming the Christian message.[7] As White aptly states, "It's simply a cultural reality that people in a post-Christian world are genuinely incredulous that

---

3. McDill, *12 Essential Skills*, conclusion, para. 8.

4. Unless otherwise noted, all Scripture quotations are from the *The Holy Bible: New King James Version* (Nashville: Thomas Nelson, 1982).

5. Robinson, *Biblical Preaching*, chap. 1, para. 11.

6. White, *Meet Generation Z*, 11.

7. Carson, *The Gagging of God*, 13–56. See also, Gentry, "Knowing the Savior."

anyone would think like . . . well, a Christian—or at least, what it means in their minds to think like a Christian."[8]

Therefore, beyond simply preaching biblical messages, what a pastor preaches may regularly need to include apologetic content, be it explicit or implicit.[9] Pastors who preach should expect to engage in various forms of apologetic encounters—helping answer challenges to belief posed by unbelievers while also helping strengthen the faith of believers. What a pastor should do and what a pastor can do, though, are not necessarily the same when it comes to apologetics, and this reveals a fundamental problem: pastors may have little knowledge of apologetics in general, and less in how apologetics relates to preaching. For those pastors who do have knowledge of apologetics, they may not know how to integrate apologetics into their ministry of preaching in a manner that avoids turning sermons into dense apologetics lectures or trite and simplistic messages lacking relevant depth and substance.

However, all Christians, including pastors, should be jealous for the character of God. The psalmist declares that "great is the LORD, and greatly to be praised" (Ps 48:1), and "give thanks to the LORD, for He is good" (Ps 106:1). In unison with Job, God's people should possess a resolve and trust that proclaims, despite appearances to the contrary, "Blessed be the name of the LORD" (Job 1:21). Yet, it is precisely God's greatness and goodness that are under attack directly and indirectly in some challenges presented by antagonists of the Christian faith.[10] If God is great, the skeptic asks, then why are there so many examples of slavery in the Bible, and why would he order the slaughter of Canaanite women and children? If God is good, the struggling Christian wonders, then why did individuals kill thousands of innocent people in the attacks on the World Trade Center on September 11, 2001, and why do earthquakes and tsunamis kill thousands in different parts of the world? These are challenging questions that strike at the very

---

8. White, *Meet Generation Z*, 130.

9. Zacharias and Geisler, *Is Your Church Ready?* 15–24.

10. Examples of such antagonism include Dawkins, *The God Delusion*; Harris, *Letters to a Christian Nation*; and Hitchens, *God is Not Great*.

heart of God's character, and the Christian message offers answers that reflect sensitivity to the issues and certainty regarding God's greatness and goodness more than anything else. Preaching can and should help with these challenges to God's character.

Believers are also commanded to "sanctify the Lord God in [their] hearts, and always be ready to give a defense to everyone who asks [them] a reason for the hope that is in [them], with meekness and fear" (1 Pet 3:15). The word translated "defense" in this verse is from the Greek *apologia*, the basis for the English word "apologetics."[11] Thus, in these few words from Peter the apostle, a command comes forth that all believers are to be ready to engage in apologetics as opportunities arise. When might a Christian business executive have opportunity to do apologetics? What about the Christian construction worker on the jobsite: what are his opportunities for apologetics? What about the Christian mother of preschoolers attending a weekly playgroup at the city park: what is her apologetic obligation? Though the details of each of these situations vary, the common theme is that each Christian is to take whatever his or her opportunities are and engage in apologetics when appropriate. What are the pastor's opportunities? He has an important platform from which his apologetic engagement could occur each week as he stands to preach to his congregation. If he is aware of particular apologetic opportunities—challenges to faith in the public media, common objections heard when evangelizing, or something specific to the local community—these are his opportunities, and if he is faithful to Peter's command, he will take them. Faithful Christians prepare for and engage in apologetics, pastors included.[12]

---

11. Zodhiates, *The Complete Word Study Dictionary*, 232.

12. Though beyond the scope of consideration here, I tentatively conclude that apologetics and preaching may even serve a concomitant role in the new heavens and new earth, since glorified humanity will still retain a rational-affective capacity which will allow for continued growth in godliness without the constraints of sin. Even without sin, apologetic proclamation could be a means to God's continued work in the redeemed of the ages. There may be hints of this in what Revelation describes as the courtroom-like worship scenes (e.g., chapter 5) where argumentation is involved in explaining to the worshipers

Introduction

Yes, I've Been There

I am increasingly convinced that a divide is developing among the types of young men entering pastoral ministry. On the one hand, there are those aspirants and new preachers who understand that their calling is to find ways to clearly communicate the gospel message and overcome obstacles to belief, and that apologetics is necessary in that process. These preachers believe in the value of apologetics but need training in how to integrate apologetics into preaching—my goal is to help them do just that. On the other hand, there are some entering the pastoral ministry who place relevance and relationality above all other concerns, which leads them to attempt to soften what they think are hard truths in the Bible and to round-off what they view as sharp corners in the exclusivity of the Christian message. Younger preachers concerned with relevance and relationality may conclude that apologetics represents the passé and archaic, the tools of a less informed and less effective generation of preachers—my hope is to challenge such preachers and help them see their views are faulty and dangerous.[13]

As a preacher for over thirty-five years, I have experienced first-hand the challenges posed by skeptics, seekers, and doubting Christians. I have also witnessed how apologetic content in preaching can and often is a powerful tool used by the Holy Spirit to clarify the thoughts, convict the hearts, and confirm the faith of those who hear the message preached. Likewise, as a student of apologetics and homiletics in formal academic settings and as a personal area of interest and study, I have learned the value of

---

what is happening and why the Lamb is worthy, etc. Certainly, there is substance enough here for at least considering the possibility.

13. I have encountered both types of preachers in my role as teacher/director in a church-based ministry training academy for the last two decades. The second type of preacher is usually influenced by concerns and methods akin to the Emergent Church movement and has uncritically adopted its ethos. For more on the Emergent Church from the perspective of its advocates, see McLaren, *A New Kind of Christian*, and *A New Kind of Christianity*; Gibbs and Bolger, *Emerging Churches*; and Anderson, *An Emergent Theology*. For a critical assessment of the Emergent Church movement, see Carson, *Becoming Conversant with the Emerging Church*.

apologetic content in sermons. Apologetics can bolster the reasonableness and effectiveness of preaching, helping to make the message of God as clear and accessible as possible. In this regard, I think there are a few fundamental ways apologetics helps preaching. Though I offer more specifics in later chapters, it will help to take a moment and discuss these right now—what I refer to as the general ways in which apologetics are a handmaiden to the pulpit.

Handmaiden to the Pulpit: General Ways Apologetics Helps Preaching

Though not an exhaustive listing, the three general ways I have found apologetics as servant to the pulpit are: 1) by helping overcome obstacles to faith in evangelistic preaching; 2) by helping overcome doubt among believers as a part of equipping them to grow as disciples; and 3) by adding overall depth to the pastor's ministry.

Overcoming Obstacles to Faith in Evangelistic Preaching

In evangelistic preaching, obstacles to belief can be based on rational and passional barriers formed when a person is ignorant of the coherence and defensibility of the Christian message.[14] Apologetic content in evangelistic preaching can help overcome such barriers to belief by addressing common objections to the Christian faith. For example, the central doctrine of the Christian faith is arguably the resurrection of Jesus (1 Cor 15:12–19). However, since the first reports of the resurrection were made to Jewish and Roman authorities, there have been attempts to disprove the claim (Matt 28:11–15).[15]

---

14. For a discussion of the concomitance of rational and passional (i.e., affective) components in faith formation, see Wainwright, *Reason and the Heart*, 1–13.

15. Justin Martyr (ca. AD 155) also states that in his day the Jewish leaders were still claiming that the disciples stole Jesus' body. See "Dialogue with Trypho,."

Introduction

Each generation of Christians since Christ resurrected has also encountered detractors from the resurrection, and this generation of believers is no different. A recent survey in Great Britain concerning beliefs about the resurrection reveals that, of the 2,010 adults surveyed, 50 percent do not believe the resurrection happened, and of the respondents identified as active Christians, 43 percent do not accept the biblical account of the resurrection as accurate.[16] Thus, when preaching a gospel message that is dependent upon the doctrine of the resurrection, the evangelistic preacher should anticipate that many in his audience likely reject the doctrine, and proactively defend it as part of a cumulative case supporting the Christian gospel.

Overcoming Doubt and Equipping Believers in Discipleship Preaching

In discipleship preaching, besetting doubts and answers to attacks on the faith of Christians by an unbelieving world can be addressed by including apologetic content in sermons. Through apologetic preaching for discipleship, believers can better overcome their own doubts (cf. Heb 11:1–2) and "contend earnestly for the faith which was once for all delivered to the saints" (Jude 3). For example, as the barrage of writing from the New Atheists demonstrates—including the frequently vitriolic and one-sided attacks upon Christianity by Sam Harris, Richard Dawkins, and Daniel Dennett—Christians are often susceptible to challenges based on a lack of preparation to answer apologetically oriented questions.[17] Believers might be harangued by opponents of the faith with questions such as: "How could a loving God command the genocide of the Canaanites?" or "How could anyone believe a Bible that was assembled in the early third century by misogynistic, power-hungry men in league with Constantine and bent on

---

16. "Resurrection Did Not Happen, Say Quarter of Christians," BBC News.

17. For a brief, scholarly overview of the New Atheists and their teachings, see Internet Encyclopedia of Philosophy, s.v. "The New Atheists," https://www.iep.utm.edu/n-atheis/.

controlling people?"[18] I know from personal experience with my own congregation that an accessible series of apologetic-infused messages targeting believers and addressing such concerns can provide great strength and resources to a struggling congregation. Such messages can also buoy the pastor's spirit amid the persistent concerns and doubts raised by those he shepherds.

Adding Overall Depth to the Pastor's Ministry Abilities

In both apologetic preaching for evangelism and for discipleship, the preacher will spend considerable time learning apologetic content and preparing it in such a way as to make it accessible through his preaching. As this happens, the preacher's apologetic knowledge and abilities increase and will usually overflow into his broader pastoral ministry. For example, learning apologetics concerning which theodicies are most helpful in addressing the problem of evil provides a pastor with greater ability to offer pastoral counsel when someone is looking for answers to personal or societal tragedies.[19] Likewise, when a pastor becomes better equipped with apologetics in his preaching, he is likely to show an increase in confidence related to evangelism, and, in turn, become more intentional about evangelizing and encouraging his congregation to do the same. As he does so, it is reasonable to think that the same apologetics that helped his confidence rise will also become a focal point in teaching others to evangelize.

---

18. Questions such as these are addressed in Copan and Craig, *Contending with Christianity's Critics*, and Craig and Meister, *God is Great*.

19. Admittedly, apologetics may not always be apropos for pastoral counseling, especially since sometimes people simply need to vent their pain, and no answers will matter. However, there are times when counselees move beyond venting and need answers in the counseling room. At these moments, apologetics can be a helpful counseling tool, even if it first comes in the form of sermons. Regarding the importance of pastoral care and preaching, see Oden, *Ministry through Word and Sacrament*, 28–57.

Introduction

A Few Helpful Definitions

To aid in navigating the chapters that follow, I offer a few key definitions related to the topic of preaching and apologetics. The definitions are composites developed from my research, and there is a certain fluidity of application assumed with each one, such that not all the aspects of the definition are necessarily relevant to each use of the term when used in the chapters that follow. The terms are: *preaching, evangelistic preaching* or *preaching as evangelism, discipleship preaching* or *preaching as discipleship, apologetics, moral apologetics, deduction, induction,* and *abduction*.

1. *Preaching*, as based upon its presentation in the Old and New Testaments, is the proclamation of God's message to believers and unbelievers.[20] Sometimes preaching is referred to or associated with declaration, exhortation, instruction, evangelism, teaching, or similar terms.[21]

2. *Evangelistic preaching* or *preaching as evangelism* is preaching focused specifically on presenting the good news of salvation by grace through faith in Christ alone to skeptics and seekers. The goal of evangelistic preaching is seeing others come into a saving relationship with God.[22]

---

20. Old Testament references to preaching include Neh 8:1–8, Jonah 1:1–2, Isa 52:7 and 61:1–3. Hebrew words associated with preaching include "*quohelet*, 'preacher;' *basar*, 'to tell good news;' *qara*, 'to call or proclaim;' [and] *qeria*, 'preaching.'" Elwell, *Evangelical Dictionary*, s.v. "Preach, Preaching." New Testament references to preaching include 1 Tim 4:13 and 2 Tim 4:2–5. Greek words include *kerysso*, proclaim; *euangelizo*, make a good announcement; *katangello*, preach; *anangello*, proclaim; and *didasko*, to teach. Fabarez, *Preaching That Changes Lives*, 7–8.

21. Brian Chapell explains, "The goal of preaching is not merely to impart information but to provide the means of transformation ordained by a sovereign God that will affect the lives and destinies of eternal souls committed to the preacher's spiritual care." Chapell, *Christ-Centered Preaching*, 2. For additional definitions of preaching that are consonant with the one I present here, compare Johnson, *The Glory of Preaching*, 7; Keller, *Preaching*, introduction, para. 4; McDill, *12 Essential Skills*, "Understanding Design," para. 3; and Vibert, *Excellence in Preaching*, 15.

22. This definition is adapted from Richard, *Preparing Evangelistic*

Introduction

3. *Discipleship preaching* or *preaching as discipleship* is preaching focused specifically on presenting Scripture to believers "for doctrine, for reproof, for correction, for instruction in righteousness" (2 Tim 3:16).[23] The goal of discipleship preaching is to aid the community of followers of Christ in knowing and doing the will of God.

4. *Apologetics* is the reasoned presentation of the truths of the Christian faith, including positive (i.e., proactively presenting reasons to believe the Christian message) and negative (i.e., answering attacks on the Christian message) presentations.[24] When conducted with unbelievers, the goal of apologetics is aiding in leading a skeptic or seeker to Christ, and when conducted with believers, the goal of apologetics is strengthening the faith of one already converted to Christ.

5. *Moral apologetics* involve either positively or negatively making an argument for the existence of God derived from the existence of objective moral facts and their implications for

---

Sermons, 72–73. Richard explains, "The New Testament uses a key word that cannot refer to anything but evangelistic proclamation, a word that can be easily transliterated from Greek: *euangelizomai*. While the other words for proclamation can include a range of content—evangelistic or not (see Paul's overlap in Rom. 16:25)—*euangelizomai* cannot bear any other meaning than the content, quality, and strategy of preaching centered on the Good News concerning Jesus." Richard, *Preparing Evangelistic Sermons*, 64. Thus, when evangelism is conducted concomitantly with preaching, it is an expression of sharing the good news through proclamation by a preacher.

23. James Stalker's description of preaching to disciples is especially apropos relative to discipleship preaching: "This is [the preacher's] work; the Book is put into [his] hands today, that [he]may unfold its contents to [his] people, conveying them into their minds by all possible avenues and applying them to all parts of their daily life." Stalker, *The Preacher and His Models*, 273–74. As John Baird explains, this type of preaching is associated with "the orderly public instruction of believers in worship based upon the Scriptures . . . that God's people may have help with daily life." Elwell, *Evangelical Dictionary*, s.v. "Preach, Preaching."

24. The distinction between negative and positive apologetics is adapted from Nash, *Faith and Reason*, 14–15. Both approaches to apologetics intend to "clear away the debris of doubt and skepticism in order to make a path for the gospel to be heard." Chatraw and Allen, *Apologetics at the Cross*, 17.

the existence of a moral being whose character and commands provide the basis for those facts.[25]

6. *Deduction* in logical discourse refers to an argument that guarantees the truth of its conclusion if the premises are also true. Accordingly, "In a deductive argument . . . if the premises are true, then it would be impossible for the conclusion to be false."[26]

7. *Induction* in logical discourse refers to an argument whose premises are presented as true, but, rather than insisting that the conclusion must also be true, the goal of induction is to affirm that "it would be unlikely that the conclusion is false."[27]

8. *Abduction* in logical discourse refers to attempts to make an argument leading to a conclusion that is considered an inference to the best explanation. Abduction's goal is less ambitious than deductive certainty or inductive near-certainty. Rather, abduction relies on the cumulative implications of the explanatory power of certain evidence in pointing toward a particular outcome as the means to make a case.[28]

What Are My Assumptions?

I have a few assumptions guiding my presentation. I share them here so that, even if you don't agree with some of my conclusions, you will at least have a better sense of where I come from theologically and practically. Regarding my theological position, I come from within historic evangelical Christianity, including the following distinctives regarding Scripture and salvation:[29] 1)

---

25. Baggett and Walls, *God and Cosmos*, chap. 9.

26. Internet Encyclopedia of Philosophy, s.v. "Deductive and Inductive Arguments," https://www.iep.utm.edu/ded-ind/.

27. Internet Encyclopedia of Philosophy, s.v. "Deductive and Inductive Arguments," https://www.iep.utm.edu/ded-ind/.

28. Baggett and Baggett, *The Morals of the Story*, 51.

29. For a detailed discussion of historic evangelical Christian beliefs, see Dorman, *A Faith for All Seasons*; Geisler, *Systematic Theology*; and Lewis and

Introduction

the Bible containing the sixty-six books of the Protestant canon is the verbally and plenarily inspired, inerrant, and infallible Word of God, the final rule of all matters of faith and practice, and in no way does the Bible ever contradict itself; and 2) salvation is by "grace through faith, [which is] the gift of God, not of works" (Eph 2:8), and only found in Jesus Christ, who is "the way, the truth and the life ... [and] no one comes to the Father except through [him]" (John 14:6).

Further, I believe that the goal of apologetics is never to simply win an argument, but always to honor God and his word. Apologetics serves to help remove obstacles to repentance and faith among unbelievers, and to strengthen the faith of believers. Likewise, apologetics is the calling of every Christian, not just a select few, and apologetics is not primarily an academic exercise but a matter of explaining one's faith amid difficulty and suffering (cf. 1 Pet 3:13–17), though there is a special role for apologetics within preaching. However, I do not spend much time on apologetic methodology regarding comparing or contrasting classical or evidential or other methods for conducting apologetics—I do have my own convictions, but the topic of methods is beyond my intentions here.

Let's Get to It

Well, we're off on a journey into the relationship between preaching and apologetics. I know that when I travel, I like to know where I am going whenever possible. Same with my writing—I like to make clear where I am heading with my reader. So, here is where we are going in the chapters that follow: chapter 1 discusses apologetics and preaching in the realm of evangelism; chapter 2 looks into apologetics and preaching in the realm of discipleship; chapter 3 focuses on the special relationship between preaching and moral apologetics; in chapter 4 we will consider how to make arguments in apologetic preaching; and in chapter 5 I offer a model

---

Demarest, *Integrative Theology*.

for those interested in how to develop apologetic sermons. If I am successful, I will help you see that there is a rational, biblical basis regarding the importance of preaching and apologetics as they relate to evangelism and discipleship. I will also help you understand why moral apologetics is especially important in apologetic preaching, and how making a cumulative case abductive argument can serve well in bringing together preaching and apologetics. Finally, the STEPS model I present helps take the guesswork out of moving from the possible to the actual for those convinced that they should integrate apologetics into their preaching. Enough introduction. Let's get to it.

CHAPTER 1

Helping Seekers Find

Apologetic Preaching and Evangelism

In this chapter, our focus now turns to an exploration of the first of two types of apologetic preaching—apologetic preaching as evangelism. I will offer three distinctives of this type of preaching, as well as a consideration of Paul's practice of apologetic preaching as evangelism in Acts 17. However, before considering a few of the distinctives of apologetic preaching as evangelism, it will help to review the definition of evangelistic preaching offered in the introduction. Evangelistic preaching, or preaching as evangelism, is preaching focused specifically on presenting the good news of salvation by grace through faith in Christ alone to skeptics and seekers with the goal of seeing them come into a saving relationship with God. In relating evangelism to apologetics, the priority is to understand that evangelism is the goal toward which apologetics is a means. Though evangelism may occur without apologetics, when apologetics is used with unbelievers the goal should be oriented toward evangelism.

Now to a discussion of the three distinctives that I think make apologetic preaching as evangelism such a powerful tool in the preacher's arsenal. The distinctives are:

1. Engaging the unbeliever's worldview
2. Employing a word-and-deed approach
3. Utilizing multiple mediums to communicate the gospel

Please remember that the point apologetic preaching as evangelism is never simply about besting an opponent or winning an argument. Rather, apologetic preaching for the sake of evangelism is about seeing seekers and skeptics come to seriously consider the good news of God's offer of salvation. Winning a soul, not an argument, is the goal of apologetic preaching as evangelism.

Engaging the Unbeliever's Worldview

Apologetic preaching as evangelism is an attempt to engage the worldview of a seeker or skeptic. "Worldview" refers to the philosophical, religious, and cultural beliefs that coalesce to provide a lens through which a person views the world around them. Sire explains that a worldview answers the following questions: "What is prime reality—the really real? What is the nature of external reality, that is, the world around us? What is a human being? What happens to a person at death? Why is it possible to know anything at all? How do we know what is right and wrong? What is the meaning human history? What personal, life-orienting commitments are consistent with this worldview?"[1]

Regarding preaching with worldview in mind, Keller explains that the evangelistic preacher's calling is to identify and relevantly apply the gospel to the "baseline cultural narratives" of a particular audience.[2] Doing so takes into consideration the following commitments on the part of the one doing apologetic preaching as evangelism: the preacher must know how the Christian worldview answers the questions related to all worldviews; he needs to determine how to approach each worldview question/aspect with a view to tying the presentation in with the gospel (i.e., asking, "How

---

1. Sire, *The Universe Next Door*, 21–23.
2. Keller, *Preaching*, chap. 5, para. 7.

does the gospel apply to this particular concern/cultural narrative about the worldview question being considered?"); and he should respectfully engage the hearer's worldview, remembering that the hearer is usually unaware of the problems with his worldview, or that Christianity has anything substantive to say regarding that worldview.

Concerning the likelihood that the average seeker or skeptic is ignorant of the relevance of Christianity, Keller laments that "religion is now almost the enemy. That is why for many today religious faith seems so unimaginable as to be crazy . . . Science and objective reason, it is said, have subtracted God from the imagination of modern people and left behind secularity."[3] Preachers are certainly called to enter into this context and offer the Christian message in the form of apologetic preaching for evangelism, but doing so requires preparation and a persisting consciousness of the importance of worldview.

Employing a Word-and-Deed Approach

The adage that the gospel needs hands and feet as well as a voice is certainly apropos when it comes to apologetic preaching as evangelism. To be sure, nothing replaces the preached word—no commitment to social justice, or humanitarian efforts, or benevolent sacrifices will ever replace the gospel as "the power of God to salvation for everyone who believes" (Rom 1:17). However, as Ken Wytsma's and Rick Gerhardt's insights reveal, the biblical approach to apologetics includes an element of servanthood and practicality that goes beyond making claims and presenting arguments. "For most people," they write, "the truth of any worldview is logically linked to practical applications. If Christianity is—as its apologists claim—the accurate understanding of reality, then it ought

---

3. Keller, *Preaching*, chap. 5, para. 7–8. The latter part of Keller's statement reflects the influence of Taylor, *A Secular Age*, 22. See also Loscalzo, *Apologetic Preaching*.

to result in practices that offer hope and solutions to the obvious brokenness of our world."[4]

What does this type of word and deed approach to apologetics consist of? One need look no further than the nascent Christian community described in Acts 2:42–47 to find an example of the concomitance of word and deed in the wake of apologetic preaching for evangelism. Luke explains that the believers "had all things in common, and sold their possessions and goods, and divided them among all, as anyone had need" (Acts 2:44–45), and that the believers were "breaking bread from house to house, [eating] their food with gladness and simplicity of heart" (Acts 2:46). What was the result of these two activities—benevolent giving to meet the needs of others and simple living in community? Luke describes the results as follows, "Having favor with all the people. And the Lord added to the church daily those who were being saved" (Acts 2:47).[5] Luke is not describing some form of Christian socialism or Christian communism. The giving was voluntary and need-based, and there is no indication in the text that owning private property was discouraged.[6] However, the Christian message was being preached and practiced as evidence of the gospel's transformative power—proof of a word-and-deed approach.

While there are certainly those occurrences in the early church that are descriptive rather than prescriptive (e.g., the way the Holy Spirit came on separate groups of people), this account of the church's practice is both descriptive and prescriptive. The church that preaches the gospel with evangelistic and apologetic

---

4. McDowell, *A New Kind of Apologist*, 62.

5. For a thorough background and exegesis of this passage, see Polhill, *Acts*, 118–22.

6. Commenting on the benevolence of the nascent Christian community, Polhill states, "Verse 45 . . . speaks against the early Christian community adopting a practice of community ownership. The imperfect tense is used, indicating that this was a recurrent, continuing practice: their practice was to sell their property and goods and apportion the proceeds whenever a need arose. This is much more in keeping with the Old Testament ideal of community equality, of sharing with the needy so that 'there will be no poor among you' (Deut. 15:4)." Polhill, *Acts*, 120.

zeal—one must recall that the primary audience to the preaching were Jews who required a clear and convincing apologetic regarding Jesus as Messiah—will support that preaching with practical acts of service and social concern.[7] Word is primary in apologetic preaching for evangelism, but deed is a vital corollary that helps incarnate the preached message.

Utilizing Multiple Mediums to Communicate

How should the one engaged in apologetic preaching for evangelism choose to communicate the gospel message? This is not a question of whether preaching should be replaced with some other medium such as drama or movies or song. Rather, this is a question of what types of content provide the best mediums to convey the gospel in an apologetic evangelistic sermon. Before considering a few possibilities, it will help to clarify why the discussion of mediums is important. Mediums relate to the broader question of how people best receive information, especially information that makes claims about absolute truth in the contemporary postmodern milieu. Commenting on the challenge of doing apologetics today, Markos states that "post moderns yearn to break out of the box in search of mystery, wonder, and awe. As a result, they tend to privilege intuition, imagination, and synthesis over logic, reason, and analysis."[8]

The challenge the apologist faces is how to appreciate and tap into these ways of relating while still holding true to the core message of the gospel. One extreme is to sacrifice everything on the altar of relevance, and another is to refuse to adapt the methods to current needs for fear of compromising the message. Neither of these two options reflect the dynamic of incarnation seen in Scripture and exemplified in the person and work of Jesus Christ, who "became flesh and dwelt among us" (John 1:14).[9] There must

---

7. As a historic example of the power of word and deed in apologetic preaching for evangelism, see Hunter, *The Celtic Way of Evangelism*, 14–24.

8. Markos, *Apologetics for the 21st Century*, 195.

9. An example of this type of incarnational ministry is Paul's description

be a way, however, to reach a culture where it is and how it thinks and relates with the ageless message of the gospel.

This is where apologetic preaching for evangelism can benefit from the works of such notable authors as G. K. Chesterton and C. S. Lewis, who both captured the imagination and heart of their respective generations by using mediums like fiction to present the core teachings of Christianity. What reader will forget Aslan as a type of Christ in Lewis's *Chronicles of Narnia*, or the impish man who was transformed when the angel killed the creature depicting lust in Lewis's *The Great Divorce*? Likewise, any reader of Chesterton's fiction will recognize that he masterfully wove themes of good and evil, mercy and forgiveness, and reason and faith into his *Father Brown Mysteries*. Does this mean that the one engaged in apologetic preaching for evangelism must become a master writer? Of course not, but it will likely help his preaching if he learns to use imagination and supposal and metanarratival story elements to reach his audience.[10]

Admittedly, there is much to learn in this area, and there may be evangelicals who consider such approaches syncretistic and instances of compromise, but even a brief perusal of Jesus' preaching reveals his use of means to capture the imagination and wonder of his hearers in familiar ways. "A sower went out to sow" (Matt 13:3), and, "The kingdom of heaven is like a certain king who wanted to settle accounts with his servants" (Matt 18:23) are two examples of Jesus' use of imaginative language for the sake of reaching an audience. The history of preaching is replete with similar examples of preachers using various means to communicate the gospel in a relevant manner, and the one who practices apologetic preaching for evangelism today should expect to do the same.

---

in 1 Cor 9:22–23 of his willingness to "become all things to all men . . . for the gospel's sake."

10. For a discussion of the role of metanarrative in reaching post-modern audiences, see Erickson, *Truth or Consequences*, 273–88.

Helping Seekers Find

Apologetic Preaching as Evangelism in Acts 17:16–32

Having considered the distinctives of apologetic preaching as evangelism, it is appropriate to turn to the text of Scripture to see if an example of such preaching is present. One such example does exist in the message Paul delivered to the philosophers and others gathered on Mars Hill in Athens, as recorded in Acts 17:16–32.[11]

> 16 Now while Paul waited for them at Athens, his spirit was provoked within him when he saw that the city was given over to idols. 17 Therefore he reasoned in the synagogue with the Jews and with the Gentile worshipers, and in the marketplace daily with those who happened to be there. 18 Then certain Epicurean and Stoic philosophers encountered him. And some said, "What does this babbler want to say?" Others said, "He seems to be a proclaimer of foreign gods," because he preached to them Jesus and the resurrection. 19 And they took him and brought him to the Areopagus, saying, "May we know what this new doctrine is of which you speak? 20 For you are bringing some strange things to our ears. Therefore we want to know what these things mean." 21 For all the Athenians and the foreigners who were there spent their time in nothing else but either to tell or to hear some new thing. 22 Then Paul stood in the midst of the Areopagus and said, "Men of Athens, I perceive that in all things you are very religious; 23 for as I was passing through and considering the objects of your worship, I even found an altar with this inscription: TO THE UNKNOWN GOD. Therefore, the One whom you worship without knowing, Him I proclaim to you: 24 God, who made the world and everything in it, since He is Lord of heaven and earth, does not dwell in temples made with hands. 25 Nor is He worshiped with men's hands, as though He needed

---

11. Similar instances of apologetic evangelistic preaching include Peter before the Sanhedrin in Acts 4, Peter at Cornelius's house in Acts 10, and Paul at the synagogue in Pisidian Antioch in Acts 13. In each instance the presentation of Christ's deity, death, and resurrection (i.e., the gospel) are followed by some type of "so what" question to address why the gospel matters.

anything, since He gives to all life, breath, and all things. 26 And He has made from one blood every nation of men to dwell on all the face of the earth, and has determined their preappointed times and the boundaries of their dwellings, 27 so that they should seek the Lord, in the hope that they might grope for Him and find Him, though He is not far from each one of us; 28 for in Him we live and move and have our being, as also some of your own poets have said, 'For we are also His offspring.' 29 Therefore, since we are the offspring of God, we ought not to think that the Divine Nature is like gold or silver or stone, something shaped by art and man's devising. 30 Truly, these times of ignorance God overlooked, but now commands all men everywhere to repent, 31 because He has appointed a day on which He will judge the world in righteousness by the Man whom He has ordained. He has given assurance of this to all by raising Him from the dead." 32 And when they heard of the resurrection of the dead, some mocked, while others said, "We will hear you again on this matter."

Though it is beyond my current concern to provide a detailed exegesis of the passage, there are points to consider regarding the text in relation to apologetic preaching as evangelism: Paul's motivation for the message he delivered; his use of common ground in introducing his message; his appropriation of natural theology and cultural elements in his message; and his segue to the gospel and an appeal to the audience at the conclusion of his message.

Paul's Motivation

What motivated Paul when he came to Athens was what would eventually lead to his opportunity to preach on Mars Hill. According to v. 16, when Paul arrived in Athens "his spirit was provoked within him when he saw that the city was given over to idols," and this led him to act and to begin preaching apologetically for the sake of evangelism. "Therefore he reasoned in the synagogue with the Jews and with the Gentile worshipers, and in the marketplace

Helping Seekers Find

daily with those who happened to be there [and] he preached to them Jesus and the resurrection" (vv. 17–18). Notice the connection between what Paul felt and what Paul did—he felt anger over the idolatry of the city, and he made an impassioned argument to Jews and Gentiles for the divinity of Jesus and his resurrection.[12] Thus, relative to apologetic preaching for evangelism Paul demonstrates his awareness of the culture he is serving, is motivated by concern for its spiritual darkness, and takes specific action in ways appropriate to each of his audiences.

Paul's Use of Common Ground

After Paul begins by connecting with the audiences he relates to in the Jewish synagogue and the marketplace (v. 17), he eventually is invited to speak to a group of Epicurean and Stoic philosophers assembled on Mars Hill (vv. 18–19).[13] They are curious about what they hear Paul preaching about Jesus and the resurrection and conclude, "He seems to be a proclaimer of foreign gods" (v. 18). Paul makes his way to the designated place for delivering his message, noticing along the way the numerous idols and altars, and begins his message by saying, "Men of Athens, I perceive that in all things you are very religious; for as I was passing through and considering the objects of your worship, I even found an altar with the inscription: TO THE UNKNOWN GOD. Therefore, the One whom you worship without knowing, Him I proclaim to you" (vv. 22–23). Paul shared a common religious interest with the Athenians, and he exploited it for the sake of the gospel. Commenting on Paul's approach in this passage, Bock observes that "here we see a key way to introduce the Christian message for an audience

---

12. The phrase "was provoked" in v. 16 translates the Greek *paroxyno*, infuriated; and the word "reasoned" in seventeen translates the Greek *dialegomai*, to argue, preach. Polhill, *Acts*, 365–66; Zodhiates, *The Complete Word Study New Testament*, 455.

13. As a former Pharisee, Paul would have had a strong connection with the Jews he encountered, and as a tentmaker, he would have also had awareness of the marketplace and its customs. These both helped him relate to his audience.

that is unfamiliar with the story of God's activity as revealed in Scripture. Most people believe in the existence of God and grant that we are accountable to him, providing a starting point for proclamation."[14] When the preacher turns to apologetic preaching for evangelism, following Paul's example of starting with common ground between preacher and audience is a solid first step forward with the gospel message.

Paul's Use of Natural Theology and Cultural Elements

Beginning in v. 24 and concluding in v. 29, Paul makes significant use of natural theology and cultural elements to develop his message. While some perceive this as Paul's commitment to a particular apologetic methodology (i.e., classical apologetics that first argues for the existence of God and then moves to specific Christian content[15]), the point here is that Paul made ample use of what his audience would have understood through their cultural commitments and worldview. I have written elsewhere that "out of the ten verses in Paul's message (totaling 269 words), eight [of the verses] deal with themes from general revelation ([accounting for] 218 of the 269 words)." Here is a breakdown of how Paul used natural theology and known culture in his message:

1. The human sense of the divine (*sensus divinitatis*): "in all things you are very religious" (vv. 22–23)

2. God is Creator: "who made the world" (v. 24)

3. God is sovereign: "Lord of heaven and earth" (v. 24)

4. God is not an idol: "does not dwell in temples," is not "worshiped with men's hands" (vv. 24–25); "we ought not to think the Divine Nature is like . . . something shaped by art and man's devising" (v. 29)

5. God is the source of all life: "gives to all life, breath, and all things" (v. 25)

14. Bock, "Acts," chap. 5, sect. "The God who made the world (17:24)."
15. Gentry, "Unleashing Faith."

6. God is the origin of all people/nations: "made from one blood every nation" (v. 26)

7. God is personal/directs history: "has determined their preappointed times" (v. 26)

8. God is immanent: "not far from each one of us" (v. 27)

9. Known poetry (culture) provides a reference to God: "as also some of your own poets have said, 'For we are also His offspring'" (v. 28)

10. God is the source and sustainer of all life: "in Him we live and move and have our being," and "we are also His offspring" (v. 28)[16]

Paul's actions regarding natural theology and culture reveal a willingness and capability on his part to find meaningful ways to deliver an apologetic evangelistic sermon in a relevant manner. He uses the metanarrative of human existence and religious impulse, what Mikeal Parsons describes as "the fullest and most dramatic speech of Paul's missionary career."[17] Preachers who preach apologetic evangelistic sermons would do well to emulate Paul in this practice.

Paul's Segue to the Gospel and Appeal to the Audience

Interestingly, Paul's message in Athens ended without much fanfare and very little explicit biblical content. Not that Paul did not share the gospel on Mars Hill, but his presentation appears rather truncated and even pithy. He segues to the gospel by declaring that God "commands all men everywhere to repent, because He has

---

16. Adapted from Gentry, "Unleashing Faith," 167–68. Based on Paul's use of natural theology and cultural ideas, as well as the location of the message, a reasonable case can be made that Paul's experience has a parallel in the trial of Socrates, also accused of introducing new gods; a key difference is between Paul's reference to the "times of ignorance" now ending, whereas Socrates spoke of them as continuing in his day. See Baggett and Baggett, *The Morals of the Story*, 17–29; and Parsons, *Acts*, part 3, "Acts 17:16—18:17," para. 8.

17. Parsons, *Acts*, part 3, "Acts 17:16—18:17," para. 9.

appointed a day on which He will judge the world in righteousness by the Man whom He has ordained. He has given assurance of this to all by raising Him from the dead" (vv. 30–31). With that brief presentation, his message ended with a proclamation of the resurrection, and his hearers then made one of three responses. Luke reports that "when they heard of the resurrection, some mocked while others said, 'We will hear you again on this matter.' . . . However, some men joined him and believed" (vv. 32, 34). Some hearers reject the gospel, some remain curious, and some repent and believe.

What these verses at the end of the message imply is that Paul's presentation came across in such a way that the hearers sensed there was a decision to make regarding what they heard. While not an overt example of an invitation at the conclusion of a gospel message, the basic elements are present—Paul warns of future judgment, preaches Jesus and the resurrection, and people make a decision.[18] Part of the significance of this for those preaching apologetic evangelistic messages is that no matter what the road is to get the hearers to the destination, remember that the destination is the coming judgment and Jesus and his resurrection. Also, it is helpful to remember that Paul's experience reveals that even the best apologists preach evangelistic sermons that receive mixed responses, so leave the responses to "God who gives the increase" (1 Cor 3:7).

---

18. For a discussion of the theological content of the gospel invitation, see Streett, *The Effective Invitation*, 37–53. Streett's work also includes a consideration of the various types of invitations used by Paul in Acts, revealing a diversity of practice that was adapted to each situation—sometimes the invitation was explicit and sometimes it was implied. Streett, *The Effective Invitation*, 78–79.

CHAPTER 2

Helping Believers Grow

Apologetic Preaching and Discipleship

As defined in chapter one, discipleship preaching or preaching as discipleship is preaching focused specifically on presenting Scripture to believers "for doctrine, for reproof, for correction, for instruction in righteousness" (2 Tim 3:16), so the goal of discipleship preaching, therefore, is to aid the community of followers of Christ in knowing and doing the will of God. When coupled with apologetics, such preaching serves to help believers overcome doubt and to acquire apologetic knowledge so they can better "give a reason for the hope that is in [them]" (1 Pet 3:15). As part of a complex of faith formation led by the Holy Spirit, "apologetics . . . equips the questioning or doubting Christian to find the intellectual confidence to be a wise witness to the truth of the gospel."[1] Later in this chapter I will consider how Jude provides an

---

1. Groothuis, *Christian Apologetics*, chap. 2, para. 66. Regarding doubt and the believer, there may be times when the issue involves matters of pastoral care more than apologetics, although the two need not be considered exclusively. Further, when addressing doubt, it is helpful to identify the type, what Gary Habermas explains as factual, emotional, or volitional instances of doubt. Habermas, *Dealing with Doubt*.

example of apologetic preaching as discipleship, but first, I want to highlight three distinctives of this type of preaching:

1. Removing obstacles to Christian growth
2. Teaching the "how" of apologetics
3. Aiding the pastor in guarding the flock

Removing Obstacles to Christian Growth

Growing, active Christians will inevitably experience doubts about the content of their faith or the surety of their relationship with the Lord as they grow and are tested (cf. James 1:2–8). To paraphrase Luther, the Christian cannot control the doubts that come at him any more than a man can control the birds that fly around the trees in his yard.[2] However, just as the man can take measures to keep the birds from nesting in his trees, so the Christian can take measures to keep doubt from nesting in his mind and heart. Also, if Christians are engaging their culture and sharing their faith, they will eventually encounter someone who is hostile to the faith and armed with one or more seemingly substantive arguments.

When Christians experience these challenges, apologetic preaching for discipleship can help by addressing the doubts and providing the answers to challenges to the faith. Sometimes doubt is intellectual, sometimes it is emotional, and sometimes is it a matter of refusing to believe out of rebellion.[3] Regardless of its source, apologetics through preaching can help the Christian move past doubt to faith and obedience. Habermas explains that apologetics is like a coin with two sides: one side focuses on those who are not yet Christians, and the other side focuses on those who already believe.[4] Both are legitimate roles for apologetics, and

---

2. Luther, "Controlling Your Thoughts," 67.

3. Author's notes in Gary Habermas's class APOL 910, Apologetic Methodology, Liberty University, Fall 2016.

4. Author's notes in Gary Habermas's class APOL 910, Apologetic Methodology, Liberty University, Fall 2016.

when a pastor knows this and takes seriously his responsibility to preach sermons that include apologetics, he helps his congregation grow in spiritual maturity.

Teaching the "How" of Apologetics

Like it or not, a preacher's congregation will learn how to do certain things by the way the preacher does them. For instance, how a preacher regularly explains the gospel at the time of invitation will have a pedagogical effect on the congregation over time, and they will likely explain the gospel in similar terms to what they have regularly heard the preacher use. This is not necessarily a problem if the preacher is careful of his method and cognizant that he is teaching by doing, especially in the pulpit. The upside to this phenomenon is that when it comes to apologetic preaching as discipleship, a preacher can both equip the saints with apologetic content and with apologetic presentation skills.

Though the congregation will not necessarily acquire the precision and polish of their pastor, they can learn the basics from his delivery method. This is, in part, how Augustine taught his mentees to preach and teach during his years of ministry as pastor and bishop in North Africa. Edward Smither explains that "the daily disciplines of prayer, scriptural study, and reading, as well as regular interaction with Augustine's teaching, prepared many monks for a possible future in church ministry."[5] Augustine certainly did more to train the monks he shepherded than simply preach and teach. However, they regularly heard his preaching in worship and structured teaching in various forms of colloquia.[6] Smither also reports that much of Augustine's apologetic material (e.g., against the Donatists, against Pelagius, against the Manicheans) was developed and presented in the context of training his mentees.[7] Thus, Augustine provides an excellent example of how

---

5. Smither, *Augustine as Mentor*, 146.
6. Smither, *Augustine as Mentor*, 146–48.
7. Smither, *Augustine as Mentor*, 147.

what is said in a sermon or teaching will both convey content and method to the hearers that desire to learn. Apologetic preaching for discipleship is one of the means to convey such content and methods to the people of God.

Aiding in Guarding the Flock

When pastors commit to apologetic preaching as discipleship, whether for a specific series of messages or as an ongoing practice in all messages, they are helping maintain the right and left limits of orthodoxy within the congregation.[8] This aspect of apologetic preaching is sometimes either overlooked due to the primary focus on answering criticism leveled against the faith and in helping unbelievers overcome obstacles to belief. However, faithful and regular apologetics in the pulpit sets a certain tone in the congregation, making clear that false teaching and attacks on the faith will be addressed, and biblical orthodoxy will be maintained in the spirit of speaking the truth in love for the sake of edifying and protecting the body (cf. Eph 4:11–16; Jude 3). This practice is not a guarantee against the rise of false teaching or unintentional heterodoxy among the brethren, especially since there are innumerable other ways people hear preaching and Christian content outside their local church. However, as Don Howell's study of Paul's leadership reveals, through regular preaching that explains and defends the Christian message, a congregation can and will gravitate toward consistent orthodoxy based on the "word of God [that] is living and powerful, and sharper than any two-edged sword . . . a discerner of the thoughts and intents of the heart" (Heb 4:12).[9]

---

8. Though I regularly deliver focused apologetic messages as discipleship preaching, I have grown in the practice of taking necessary apologetic excurses during messages that are not otherwise apologetic in orientation. For example, if preaching about the blessing of the resurrection vis-à-vis justification, it is likely that a side point will be offered about the reliability of the resurrection accounts in the Bible. This can be accomplished in just a few minutes, and the overall effect on the congregation and the sermon is a sense of confidence and legitimacy as the Christian message is presented as true and reliable.

9. Howell, *Servants of the Servant*, 256–64.

There is also historical support for the use of apologetics in protecting the church's doctrine. Douglas Taylor's exploration of the role of positive apologetics in the first three centuries of church history demonstrates precedent for apologetics in this role.[10] Taylor explains that through the use of apologetics the early church stood firm against encroaching heresy by offering "justification for belief in and commendation of Christianity."[11] When faced with attempts by heretics to alter "one or more aspects of the deity, death, and resurrection reports as they related to Jesus," these early apologists helped "establish the credibility of Christianity."[12] Likewise, when pastors commit to apologetic preaching today, they help believers live within a hostile culture without sacrificing their distinctive beliefs. Perhaps one of the greatest though underutilized weapons in the preacher's arsenal when it comes to doctrinal purity is the practice of regular apologetic preaching for discipleship, something we will now consider in Jude.

Apologetic Preaching as Discipleship in Jude

Jude's epistle, though only a short twenty-five verses, represents one of the clearest examples of apologetic preaching as discipleship in the entire Bible. Probably written for the purpose of being used as a sermon in churches comprised of primarily Jewish converts to Christianity,[13] Jude offers several helpful considerations regarding preaching, apologetics, and discipleship, including: his purpose; his arguments; his presentation of moral and doctrinal exposé and instruction; and his reminders to the congregation.

---

10. Taylor, "One from the Beginning."
11. Taylor, "One from the Beginning," 3.
12. Taylor, "One from the Beginning," 3.
13. "Jude offers us a sermon in rhetorical form that has only an epistolary opening to indicate that it came to the audience in a written form, though it was likely delivered orally at the point of destination. We must think constantly in terms of the oral majority of the culture and how literate persons like Jude were trying to speak into their situations." Witherington, *Letters and Homilies*, 560.

1 Jude, a bondservant of Jesus Christ, and brother of James, to those who are called, sanctified by God the Father, and preserved in Jesus Christ: 2 Mercy, peace, and love be multiplied to you. 3 Beloved, while I was very diligent to write to you concerning our common salvation, I found it necessary to write to you exhorting you to contend earnestly for the faith which was once for all delivered to the saints. 4 For certain men have crept in unnoticed, who long ago were marked out for this condemnation, ungodly men, who turn the grace of our God into lewdness and deny the only Lord God and our Lord Jesus Christ. 5 But I want to remind you, though you once knew this, that the Lord, having saved the people out of the land of Egypt, afterward destroyed those who did not believe. 6 And the angels who did not keep their proper domain, but left their own abode, He has reserved in everlasting chains under darkness for the judgment of the great day; 7 as Sodom and Gomorrah, and the cities around them in a similar manner to these, having given themselves over to sexual immorality and gone after strange flesh, are set forth as an example, suffering the vengeance of eternal fire.

8 Likewise also these dreamers defile the flesh, reject authority, and speak evil of dignitaries. 9 Yet Michael the archangel, in contending with the devil, when he disputed about the body of Moses, dared not bring against him a reviling accusation, but said, "The Lord rebuke you!" 10 But these speak evil of whatever they do not know; and whatever they know naturally, like brute beasts, in these things they corrupt themselves. 11 Woe to them! For they have gone in the way of Cain, have run greedily in the error of Balaam for profit, and perished in the rebellion of Korah. 12 These are spots in your love feasts, while they feast with you without fear, serving *only* themselves. *They are* clouds without water, carried about by the winds; late autumn trees without fruit, twice dead, pulled up by the roots; 13 raging waves of the sea, foaming up their own shame; wandering stars for whom is reserved the blackness of darkness forever.

14 Now Enoch, the seventh from Adam, prophesied about these men also, saying, "Behold, the Lord comes

with ten thousands of His saints, 15 to execute judgment on all, to convict all who are ungodly among them of all their ungodly deeds which they have committed in an ungodly way, and of all the harsh things which ungodly sinners have spoken against Him." 16 These are grumblers, complainers, walking according to their own lusts; and they mouth great swelling *words*, flattering people to gain advantage. 17 But you, beloved, remember the words which were spoken before by the apostles of our Lord Jesus Christ: 18 how they told you that there would be mockers in the last time who would walk according to their own ungodly lusts. 19 These are sensual persons, who cause divisions, not having the Spirit. 20 But you, beloved, building yourselves up on your most holy faith, praying in the Holy Spirit, 21 keep yourselves in the love of God, looking for the mercy of our Lord Jesus Christ unto eternal life.

22 And on some have compassion, making a distinction; 23 but others save with fear, pulling *them* out of the fire, hating even the garment defiled by the flesh. 24 Now to Him who is able to keep you from stumbling, and to present *you* faultless before the presence of His glory with exceeding joy, 25 to God our Savior, who alone is wise, *be* glory and majesty, dominion and power, both now and forever. Amen.

Jude's Purpose

Immediately after greeting his audience, Jude declares the reason for his writing: "Beloved, while I was very diligent to write to you concerning our common salvation, I found it necessary to write to you exhorting you to contend earnestly for the faith which was once for all delivered to the saints" (v. 3). The first part of the verse reveals Jude's pastoral intention to instruct the believers in their shared faith, and the last part reveals his pastoral concern that his focus must change to an apologetic matter ("contend earnestly") related to the Christian faith ("the faith . . . once for all delivered"). Regarding this apologetic concern, Doskocil explains that "the verb for contend earnestly (*epagonizomai*) occurs only here in the [New Testament]. It was used to describe athletes in competition striving with great intensity for victory," and that "since this faith was once for all delivered to the saints, every Christian, not just church leaders, is to defend Biblical [*sic*] truth from erroneous teachings of false teachers."[14] This second point offered by Doskocil is especially apropos when considering why Jude is urging believers to the apologetic task of "striving with great intensity"—Jude knows that apologetics is the calling of all believers, and his goal is to urge them to fulfill their calling in defense of the faith. Jude continues in v. 4 by identifying the exact nature of the apologetic concern: "Certain men have crept in unnoticed . . . ungodly men, who turn the grace of our God into lewdness and deny the only Lord God and our Lord Jesus Christ." Though discussed further below, Jude reveals the concern has a moral aspect ("ungodly men . . . lewdness") and a theological aspect ("deny the Lord God and our Lord Jesus Christ"). Thus, Jude is insistent that every believer must take up the apologetic fight with intensity in defending the common Christian doctrine and practice. Any pastor who would engage in apologetic preaching for the sake of discipleship will press upon his hearers the same concern with the same urgency. The faith must be defended.

Jude's Apologetic Arguments

Jude's arguments contain several elements related to apologetic preaching for discipleship. He makes clear that the concern is no mere secondary matter of private interpretation or personal conviction but is a direct attack on the grace of God in word and deed (vv. 4, 19). Further, with his focus identified, Jude presents a case against the teachers and their error, beginning with references to the Old Testament and apocryphal books/accounts known to the readers (vv. 5–11), thereby establishing his argument under the

---

14. Doskocil, "Jude," II.A., para. 3–4.

auspices of divine revelation and communal knowledge.[15] Jude is also adamant that there is judgment coming to the false teachers and those who follow their errors (vv. 12–15). He is addressing something that is more than a mere theoretical issue, but one with eternal significance (vv. 14–15).

Though sounding a strong warning, Jude also offers assurance to the believers that what is happening is not something to be surprised about or fear, but something that is concomitant with living in the Last Days (vv. 16–18). Finally, Jude ends his argument with a note of pastoral direction regarding helping those caught in the errors (vv. 20–23) and pastoral comfort based on the character and faithfulness of God (vv. 24–25).[16] Through the entire presentation Jude remains focused on the apologetic issue and his concern for the congregation, providing warning and consolation in the face of pernicious moral and doctrinal error.

Jude's Moral and Doctrinal Exposé and Instruction

As Jude makes his apologetic argument, he is clear to expose and instruct regarding the moral and doctrinal errors of the false teachers. In what some preachers today might find a refreshing example of pastoral authority and directness, Jude does not hesitate to use strong descriptive language to make his point: "marked out for this condemnation" (v. 4), "lewdness . . . denying the only Lord God" (v. 4), "dreamers [that] defile the flesh, reject authority, and speak evil of dignitaries" (v. 8), "like brute beasts . . . corrupt themselves" (v. 10), "Woe to them!" (v. 11), "serving only themselves . . . twice dead" (v. 12), "for whom is reserved the blackness of darkness forever" (v. 13), "ungodly sinners" (v. 15), "grumblers, complainers" (v. 16), "mockers . . . walk[ing] according to their own ungodly lusts" (v. 18), "not having the Spirit" (v. 19).

---

15. Compare Schreiner, *Jude*, 447–51, and Witherington, *Jude*, 623–25.

16. Regarding the pastoral significance of Jude's concluding doxology, Watson explains that "by ending his appeal with a focus upon God, Christ, and their future hope, his audience is ever more persuaded to act as Jude advises." Watson, *Invention, Arrangement and Style*, 76.

It is difficult to conceive that anyone who received Jude's message, including the false teachers, would be unclear on the seriousness of the moral and doctrinal sins that precipitated an apologetic sermon to warn, motivate, and instruct the brethren. This aspect of apologetic preaching for discipleship takes courage and discernment, lest the preacher go to the extreme of avoiding issues or the extreme of preaching only judgment. Paul's counsel to the Ephesians is helpful at this point: "Speaking the truth in love . . . grow up in all things into Him who is the head—Christ" (Eph 4:15).

Jude's Reminders to the Congregation

One of the striking aspects of Jude's message to the believers is his instruction to commit to "building [themselves] up in [their] most holy faith . . . keep[ing themselves] in the love of God" (vv. 20–21), and "on some have compassion . . . but others save with fear, pulling them out of the fire" (vv. 22–23). These two groupings of commands, the first directed to the believer's selfcare and the second to the believer's care of others, reveal that Jude's apologetic preaching included the expectation that the hearers would put into practice what they were taught. Yes, God keeps his people (v. 24), but this assurance is not a reason to do nothing. On the contrary, the outcome of apologetic preaching for discipleship is a better-equipped believer who knows what she believes, why she believes it, and how she must live in relation to her beliefs.

Calvin's comment on Jude's exhortation to the believers to take steps to strengthen themselves in the face of the false teachers offers a helpful insight. He explains that Jude "shews the manner in which they could overcome all devices of Satan, that is, by having love connected with faith, and by standing on their guard as it were in the watch-tower, until the coming of Christ."[17] Jude's intention is both immediate and eschatological, looking to help shore up the believers presently and until Christ returns. This is a poignant reminder that apologetic preaching for discipleship has

---

17. Calvin, "Jude," sect. "Jude 20–25."

a sense of the now-and-not-yet. As the disciple learns to defend the faith, he becomes an ambassador for Christ in this world while helping others stand firm in anticipation of the next.

Summary

The focus of this chapter has been how apologetic preaching as discipleship provides unique opportunities for the preacher, including overcoming obstacles to Christian growth, teaching the "how" of apologetics, and aiding in guarding the flock. We also discussed how Jude's epistle provides an example of apologetic preaching for discipleship in these areas based on his epistle's purpose, apologetic arguments, use of moral and doctrinal exposé and instruction, and the reminder to the congregation of their responsibilities. These points offer preachers theoretical insight and practical motivation concerning the importance of apologetics and discipleship. In the next chapter I will consider how apologetic preaching has a special relationship with moral apologetics.

CHAPTER 3

God is Good

The Special Relationship between Preaching and Moral Apologetics

Having considered the rationale for a general connection between preaching and apologetics, the next area of inquiry concerns the special role of moral apologetics within preaching. To review the definition provided in chapter 1, moral apologetics involves either positively or negatively making an apologetic argument for the existence of God derived from the existence of objective moral facts and their implications for the existence of a moral being whose character and commands provide the basis for those facts. It is helpful to point out that within moral apologetics there are moral arguments for the existence of God, and there are ways of arguing morally relative to God's existence—both are under the penumbra of moral apologetics.[1] Likewise, regarding

---

1. Specific to moral arguments, there are numerous versions available to apologists (e.g., Thomas Aquinas's version based on degrees of perfection in the *Summa Theologiae*, or C. S. Lewis's version in *Mere Christianity*), but, for reasons discussed in chapter 4 below, I prefer a version of the moral argument that is cumulative, abductive, and teleological. For a discussion of the various nuances within moral apologetics, including the distinction between moral arguments for the existence of God and arguing morally/for morality based

moral apologetics broadly conceived, there are several reasons to consider that are related to the rationale for a special affinity between preaching and moral apologetics. The reasons presented here are those I consider most pertinent to the present discussion.

Emphasizing the Moral Nature of God and Humanity

When utilizing moral apologetics in preaching, especially in evangelistic preaching, an emphasis upon the objectivity of moral facts can provide tremendous benefit in helping unbelievers consider the role of morality in pointing them to God.[2] Such moral facts include moral goodness, moral obligations, moral knowledge, moral transformation, and a sense of moral providence.[3] Consider, for example, moral obligations as a part of apologetic evangelistic preaching. It is not difficult to imagine how a preacher could speak of every person's innate sense of moral obligation as a means of revealing both God as the moral standard and each person's imperfection in keeping his or her moral obligations.

This type of use of moral apologetics in a sermon could provide the basis for an entire sermon. Even if the preacher's message is on a different topic than moral apologetics, when coming to transition to the invitation it is a fairly straightforward move to include moral obligations. These can help highlight humanity's

---

on God's existence, see Baggett and Walls, *God and Cosmos*, chaps. 4–8, and *Good God*, chaps. 1, 8–10. See also Geisler, *Christian Apologetics*, 276–77, and *Systematic Theology*, 16–33, 566–73, and 1556–62.

2. Baggett and Baggett, *The Morals of the Story*, 49.

3. Baggett and Baggett devote an entire chapter to each of these categories in *The Morals of the Story*. Moral goodness relates to the existence of things that are genuinely good, as contrasted to those that are genuinely evil. Moral obligations relate to the sense of oughtness associated with morality and moral goodness. Moral knowledge relates to man's ability to know that genuine moral goodness exists. Moral transformation relates to the awareness and experience of genuine change in a person's moral acts and abilities. Moral providence relates to man's highest good being found in a right moral relationship with God and others.

problem with sin and the need of a perfect moral savior. Further, in instances of apologetic preaching for discipleship, the universal innate sense of moral obligation provides a helpful segue to point believers to their need to trust not in their own imperfect righteous deeds but in the perfect righteousness of Jesus.[4] Indeed, the moral nature of God and humanity provides many opportunities for preaching that includes a moral apologetic component.

Centering Evangelistic Preaching on Sin, Righteousness, and Redemption

Related to the reason just discussed, but specifically focused on apologetic preaching for evangelism, the moral center of the gospel regarding sin, righteousness, and redemption also reveals a vital link between preaching and moral apologetics. Consider this point related to the categories of moral facts discussed by Baggett and Baggett: goodness, obligations, knowledge, transformation, and providence.[5] Can the gospel be preached without speaking of moral goodness, since "no one is good but God alone" (Mark 10:18)? No. Can the gospel be preached without speaking of moral obligations, since "all have sinned and fall short of the glory of God" (Rom 3:23)? No. Can the gospel be preached without speaking of moral knowledge, since "what may be known of God is manifest in [all persons] . . . His invisible attributes . . . even His

---

4. In my discipleship preaching I regularly use a sermon structure designed to emphasize the concomitance between moral apologetics (in the broader sense of arguing morally based on God's existence) and transformation. The method, one I developed in 2012–2015 while completing DMin studies, is based on the acrostic COACH: Connect to a genuine need for transformation in the believer's life, Orient the discussion of the need to the Word of God, Apply the challenge and importance of the needed transformation to specific life instances, Cultivate the proper "I can't" tension by emphasizing that the believer must look to Christ for her righteousness and moral transformation, and Heal with the gospel as applied to believers with the goal of seeing them renew their resolve to live holy while trusting wholly in Christ for their righteousness before God. This type of sermon structure may be adapted for evangelism or discipleship.

5. Baggett and Baggett, *The Morals of the Story*, chap. 5–9.

eternal power and Godhead" (Rom 1:18–20)? No. Can the gospel be preached without speaking of moral transformation, since the gospel reveals that "if anyone is in Christ, he is a new creation; old things have passed away; behold all things have become new" (2 Cor 5:17)? No. Can the gospel be preached without speaking of moral providence, since the gospel reveals that "God so loved the world that He gave His only begotten Son, that whoever believes in Him should not perish but have everlasting life" (John 3:16), even though "men loved darkness rather than light, because their deeds were evil" (John 3:19)? No.

To preach the gospel is to preach regarding moral goodness, moral obligations, moral knowledge, moral transformation, and moral providence. Of course, it is possible that someone could attempt to preach the gospel without these moral facts, but what gospel would that be? It is also possible to confuse moral facts vis-à-vis the gospel with preaching moralism as a means to salvation. Yet, such possibilities notwithstanding, anyone who takes seriously the Bible and the evangelical faith revealed therein will recognize that to preach the gospel requires preaching about moral facts.

Engaging Passional Reason

This final part of consideration concerning the rationale for the reciprocal relationship between preaching and moral apologetics is, admittedly, one that is easily overlooked in discussion of the "what" and "how" of apologetics. Apologists are stereotyped, and sometimes deservedly so, as logic choppers whose primary engagement with life is cerebral and rational. To summarize a remark from one of my parishioners during a discussion following an apologetic conference a few years ago, it is apparent that apologists have a head, but not always apparent that they have a heart. Is this a caricature? Certainly, but a caricature is a likeness to something real, albeit an exaggerated likeness. This is why it is important to remember that when apologetics is primarily cerebral and rational, it is out of balance and possibly even unbiblical.

Consider how it might be unbiblical for apologetics to become primarily cerebral and rational. In Peter's words, the purpose of apologetics is to "give a defense to everyone who asks you a reason for the hope that is in you" (1 Pet 3:15). This passage reveals, among numerous other things, that apologetics is tied to hope, the hope abiding in a Christian even in the most difficult circumstances.[6] Such hope certainly contains a rational component, but it is more than a logical process that generates and sustains hope—hope involves the whole person's mind, will, and emotions in trusting God and knowing that he will take care of his children. Thus, to engage in apologetics is to engage in more than a cerebral consideration of premises and conclusions.

Further, if apologetics is only engaged in the rational components of fact and argumentation, it is out of balance, since to be balanced in apologetics requires the passional and affective elements of a person that are associated with hope and confidence in God. Balanced apologetics engages the whole person, appealing to what Wainwright describes as passional reason, "the possession of the appropriate moral and spiritual temperament" as concomitant to reason in "track[ing] truth."[7] What Wainwright and others (e.g., Pascal) recognize is that there is a necessary relationship between a person's rational and affective capacities that come together in forming faith.[8]

---

6. For a helpful consideration of the broader context of Peter's words concerning apologetics and how they relate to the whole person and the centrality of hope in the gospel message, see Schreiner, *Jude*, 168–79.

7. Wainwright, *Reason and the Heart*, 5.

8. An example of Pascal's appeal to what Wainwright describes as passional reason with a moral apologetic bent is found in quotes like this one from Pascal's Pensees: "Men despise religion. They hate it, fear it is true. To remedy this, we must begin by showing that religion is not contrary to reason; that it is venerable, to inspire respect for it; then we must make it lovable, to make good men hope it is true; finally, we must prove it is true. Venerable, because it has perfect knowledge of man; lovable because it promises the true good." One can readily see there is also a moral component to Pascal's thought of the gospel (what he calls religion), as he speaks of the fear men have regarding its truth (with moral implications), and the possibility that good men will want it to be true, and that believers should show its truth (a reference to living as much as

How does this relate to moral apologetics and preaching? Due to the innate moral aspects of personhood (e.g., conscience, judicial sentiment), the fundamental moral consideration associated with God's existence, and the *sensus divinitatis* found within all persons, moral apologetics in preaching offers a direct method of engaging the whole person on the levels of intellect, conscience, judicial sentiment, and the sense of the divine.[9] Consider how all of these elements are present in the response of the hearers to Peter's evangelistic sermon on Pentecost, which included claims of Christ's divinity, Israel's moral culpability for rejecting him, and the possibility of change upon repentance and faith: "Now when they heard this, they were cut to the heart, and said to Peter and the rest of the apostles, 'Men and brethren, what shall we do?' Then Peter said to them, 'Repent, and let every one of you be baptized in the name of Jesus Christ for the remission of sins'" (Acts 2:37–38). Peter's preaching was clear, there is a moral component to the gospel, and the response of the hearers was also clear as they responded with mind and heart to the message. This example reveals that moral apologetics in preaching is important because it offers an opportunity for preachers to engage the passional reason of hearers in a unique, powerful manner.

Before concluding the discussion of this reason for the importance of preaching and moral apologetics, it is worth considering the relationship between moral apologetics and what has been described as an existential argument for God's existence. The form of the argument here is from Clifford Williams, author of *Existential Reasons for Belief in God: A Defense of Desires and Emotions for Faith*.[10] In syllogistic form, Williams's argument is as follows:

> P1: "We need cosmic security. We need to know that we will live beyond the grave in a state that is free from the defects of

---

argumentation) because it reveals who man is (moral implications) and what is the true good (moral implications). See Pascal, *Pensees*, 49.

9. For a discussion of conscience, judicial sentiment, and *sensus divinitatis* under the broader penumbra of a systematic theological consideration of anthropology, see Dorman, *A Faith for All Seasons*, 3–8.

10. Williams, *Existential Reasons*.

this life, a state that is full of goodness and justice. We need a more expansive life, one in which we love and are loved. We need meaning, and we need to know that we are forgiven for going astray. We need to experience awe, to delight in goodness, and to be present with those we love."

P2: "Faith in God satisfies these needs."

C: "Therefore, we are justified in having faith in God."[11]

This presentation from Williams, though not exclusively focused on moral apologetics, certainly includes key moral elements (e.g., "free from the defects of this life . . . goodness and justice . . . to know that we are forgiven for going astray . . . to delight in goodness"[12]), and those moral elements are both rational (e.g., wanting goodness and justice, and to receive forgiveness) and affective (e.g., wanting freedom from defect, and to delight in what is good). Thus, the preacher utilizing moral apologetics certainly has a powerful means at his disposal when it comes to reaching hearers via their passional reason.

Summary

In this chapter we investigated the matter of apologetic preaching and moral apologetics, specifically considering how moral apologetics aids the preacher by emphasizing the moral nature of God and humanity; by helping center evangelistic preaching on sin, righteousness, and redemption; and by engaging passional reason. In the next chapter I offer a brief overview of apologetic preaching and abductive argumentation. After discussing deductive and inductive argumentation, an example of abduction is offered concerning the moral argument for God's existence. The chapter concludes with a presentation of the rationale for arguing abductively in apologetic preaching, as well as an exploration of Joshua 24:1–25 as an example of abduction in apologetic preaching.

---

11. Williams, *Existential Reasons*, 32.
12. Williams, *Existential Reasons*, 32.

CHAPTER 4

A Reasonable Proclamation

Apologetic Preaching and Making Arguments

To make apologetic arguments is to engage, at some point, in rational argumentation. Groothuis makes a helpful observation related to this idea, stating that "apologetics means philosophical engagement, and philosophy trades in logic."[1] Thus, though logic and argumentation may be difficult for some Christians, apologetics without arguments reduces to assertions and becomes a denial of Peter's command to "be ready to give a defense" (1 Pet 3:15). Is there, though, a preferred style of argumentation for apologetics, especially apologetic preaching? While my conclusion is that all forms of valid argumentation may have a place in apologetics at some point, it is in abductive argumentation that apologetic preaching may find its greatest ally. Before making the case for why abduction is important, other types of argumentation—deduction and induction—are discussed briefly. Thereafter, abduction is illustrated, and reasons are offered for choosing abductive argumentation in apologetic preaching, as well as an example of abductive apologetic preaching from Joshua 24:1–25.

---

1. Groothuis, *Christian Apologetics*, chap. 3, para. 2.

Deductive and Inductive Argumentation

Craig explains that "in a sound deductive argument, the conclusion follows inevitably from the premises . . . the premises [must] be true and the logic [must] be valid."[2] For example, if arguing deductively for God's existence based on morality, the argument could be given as follows:

P1: If God does not exist, then objective moral values and duties do not exist.

P2: Objective moral values and duties do exist.

C: So, God exists.[3]

Craig also explains that induction "is an argument of which the premises may be true and the logical inferences valid but the conclusion still be false . . . the conclusion is quite likely true . . . but it is not inevitably true."[4] An example of an inductive argument for God's existence based on joy or desire is as follows:

P1: Creatures are not born with desires unless satisfaction for these desires exists.

P2: A baby feels hunger: well, there is such a thing as food. A duckling wants to swim: well, there is such a thing as water. Men feel sexual desire: well, there is such a thing as sex.

C: If I find in myself a desire which no experience in this world can satisfy, the most probable explanation is that I was made for another world.[5]

Both deduction and induction are options for argumentation, and a preacher whose goal is to include apologetics in preaching will benefit from learning how and when to use these approaches. Sometimes the nature of the sermon or the context may require a

---

2. Craig, *Reasonable Faith*, 52.
3. This is how Craig argues for God's existence, as presented (and critiqued) in Baggett and Walls, *God and Cosmos*, chap. 2, para. 23.
4. Craig, *Reasonable Faith*, 52–53.
5. Lewis, *Mere Christianity*, 113.

level of specificity and logical precision found in deduction. Likewise, with some topics an inductive approach may help build the confidence of the believers by presenting them with arguments that tend toward a high degree of certainty but still leave room for disagreement. In both instances the preacher will have to decide whether deduction or induction is best. However, as will be considered now, abductive argumentation also offers important benefits to apologetic preaching.

The Rationale for Arguing Abductively in Apologetic Preaching

Abductive argumentation is similar to inductive argumentation, though abduction hopes to arrive at an inference to the best explanation without claiming a standard of certainty that is unattainable, while induction claims more certainty with less concern for inference to the best explanation. Both are dissimilar to deduction, since deduction claims to come to absolute certainty if the premises and logic are valid and true. An example of abduction in arguing for God's existence based on morality could be presented as follows:

P1: Moral goodness and evil are realities in the human experience.

P2: The human experience of moral realities raises the oughtness that each person feels concerning moral obligations.

P3: Humans are aware that they experience moral realities and moral oughtness, and, therefore, humans can and do have moral knowledge.

P4: In light of the moral experience of humans—moral realities, moral oughtness, moral knowledge—there is also an experience of moral transformation that humans know intuitively and experientially.

P5: The experience of moral transformation—especially with the aforementioned experience of moral realities, moral oughtness, and moral transformation—raises the possibility that there is a moral providence, a highest moral good.

P6: That God exists and is the source of these moral facts (1–5) is a reasonable, probable conclusion.

P7: This is the claim of the Christian faith, whose description of God is consistent with these moral facts.

C: It is, therefore, a reasonable inference—conceivably the best inference based on the evidence—that the Christian God exists.[6]

For the sake of this discussion, I think abduction aligns best with the goals of apologetic preaching for the following reasons: it encourages epistemic humility in apologetic dialogue; and it helps avoid the error of oversimplification. Let's consider each of these, in turn.

Encouraging Epistemic Humility in Apologetic Dialogue

Because it claims to come to an inference to the best explanation, abduction offers a manner of apologetic reasoning in preaching that is not unnecessarily dogmatic, nor without a sense of certainty and conviction appropriate to the claims of the gospel on unbelievers and believers. As Baggett and Baggett explain, "The procedure of abduction goes like this: we come across something that needs to be explained, then we identify a range of possible explanations, and then we narrow the list down to the best one."[7] Some apologists might chafe at this approach, claiming that the apologetic enterprise should insist on certainty, and that apologetic preaching, especially, should prefer more than an inference to the best explanation as an outcome.

---

6. This is my attempt at a cumulative presentation of the arguments of Baggett and Walls, *Good God* and *God and Cosmos*; as well as Baggett and Baggett, *The Morals of the Story*.

7. Baggett and Baggett, *The Morals of the Story*, 50.

However, whereas deduction and induction (to a lesser degree) claim certainty, there is a sense in which such claims (especially in deduction) to absolute certainty lack explanatory power when it comes to how faith forms around what is "hoped for . . . [and] unseen" (Heb 11:1–2). Is the Christian worldview compelling? Absolutely. Is there evidence worthy of consideration? Of course. However, the ideas of certainty associated with argumentation are not something found in the pages of the Bible, but in the later developments of modern thought, which has a decided bias against the idea of biblical faith.[8] Abduction is a way to keep the apologist in check against the temptation to overconfidence in the power of his arguments, and to help him remember that there is more involved in coming to faith than syllogisms and rationality.

Avoiding the Error of Oversimplification

This is a problem that some apologists fall into when they think a simple syllogism is all that is needed to make the case for some aspect of Christian truth. Rather, accepting that one cannot with absolute epistemic certainty prove the existence of God and truth of Christianity, apologists may assume that their personal convictions are equivalent to philosophical standards of truth and certainty. They assume that belief is simply a matter of following the premises to the logical conclusion and expect that their hearers only need to follow the logic of an argument to come to belief in God or some other aspect of Christian truth.[9] For example, it may be tempting to think that Craig's version of the cosmological argument for God's existence is an unassailable argument that, when delivered by the apologetic preacher, brings critics of Christianity to heel by silencing their arguments. Craig's argument is as follows:

P1: Whatever begins to exist has a cause.

---

8. Baggett and Baggett, *The Morals of the Story*, 50.

9. For a discussion of the challenges of this type of thinking and presentation, and a positive case for abduction in apologetics, see Gundry and Cowan, *Five Views*, 148–50.

P2: The universe began to exist.

C: Therefore, the universe has a cause.[10]

When this approach to argumentation is assumed by an apologist to be a knock down argument that requires the unbeliever to yield to the gospel, a fundamental element is missing. Conversion is ordinarily a process that takes time and possibly numerous encounters, and it is only the exception that finds a person coming to Christ after hearing only one argument.[11] Rather, and this is one of the benefits of abductive argumentation, effective apologetic preaching takes time and a cumulative presentation that appeals to the best explanation of what is under discussion to see someone come to faith in Christ. Groothuis explains:

> How does one present an argument for the Christian worldview as the best hypothesis? The answer: carefully, slowly and piece by piece. First, the hypothesis needs to be formulated clearly. For apologetics, this means paying close attention to the components and implications of the Christian worldview, with an eye for detecting false stereotypes and caricatures. Second, identify the worldviews that are potential rivals to Christianity. These will be the worldviews that are plausible . . . one that holds interest and appeal for a significant number of people at a particular time and place . . . Plausibility should not be confused with credibility, which deals with whether or not any claim is true and rational. The credibility of a worldview is determined by whether or not arguments marshaled in its favor are compelling and logically coherent.[12]

---

10. Craig, *Reasonable Faith*, 111. This is Craig's version of the Kalam Cosmological Argument, one he regularly uses with remarkable success in debates with atheists. It is easy to mistake Craig's success with the normal response of such argumentation on an evangelistic context. Admittedly, Craig is not so much evangelizing as he is defending against high-level academic attacks.

11. For a concise discussion regarding the difference between process and moment in evangelism, see Gentry, *You Shall Be My Witnesses*, chap. 11.

12. Groothuis, *Christian Apologetics*, chap. 3, para. 14.

Among several impressions one might have from Groothuis's statement, it is not likely that anyone will conclude that what he describes is a quick or one-time process. Apologetic argumentation takes time and patience, and the abductive approach lends itself to these things more than argumentation by deduction or induction. Whereas the latter two are intended to make the conclusion a necessary outcome of the premises, abduction makes a solid case in appealing to the best explanation without forcing the conversation to a premature conclusion or impasse. Like Paul in Athens sharing the gospel on Mars Hill (Acts 17:22–34), the abductive argument in the hands of the apologetic preacher offers a reasonable explanation of the audience's circumstances while engaging their worldview and positively presenting the Christian worldview. Some may scoff, some may decide to hear more, and some may believe—whatever the outcome may be, the cumulative abductive case for faith has been made.

Abductive Apologetic Preaching in Joshua 24:1–25

In Joshua 24:1–25, Joshua delivered his second farewell address to Israel. His first address was given in vv. 1–16, and, as David Howard explains, "both were given in the pastoral, hortatory style."[13] The significance of Howard's description for the present consideration is that what Joshua did in these two addresses is essentially preach a final message to those he had led since Moses's death. The first message focused on the leaders, and the second on the whole nation of Israel. In what follows, I will evaluate Joshua's message to the nation in vv. 1–25 through the lens of apologetic preaching, specifically regarding the way he made his argument. As will be developed, Joshua's concern, his basic apologetic argument, and his invitation to the hearers provide an example of abductive apologetic preaching.

> 1 Then Joshua gathered all the tribes of Israel to Shechem and called for the elders of Israel, for their heads, for their

13. Howard, *Joshua*, chap. 4, sect. 3, para. 1.

judges, and for their officers; and they presented themselves before God. 2 And Joshua said to all the people, "Thus says the Lord God of Israel: 'Your fathers, *including* Terah, the father of Abraham and the father of Nahor, dwelt on the other side of the River in old times; and they served other gods. 3 Then I took your father Abraham from the other side of the River, led him throughout all the land of Canaan, and multiplied his descendants and gave him Isaac. 4 To Isaac I gave Jacob and Esau. To Esau I gave the mountains of Seir to possess, but Jacob and his children went down to Egypt. 5 Also I sent Moses and Aaron, and I plagued Egypt, according to what I did among them. Afterward I brought you out. 6 'Then I brought your fathers out of Egypt, and you came to the sea; and the Egyptians pursued your fathers with chariots and horsemen to the Red Sea. 7 So they cried out to the Lord; and He put darkness between you and the Egyptians, brought the sea upon them, and covered them. And your eyes saw what I did in Egypt. Then you dwelt in the wilderness a long time. 8 And I brought you into the land of the Amorites, who dwelt on the other side of the Jordan, and they fought with you. But I gave them into your hand, that you might possess their land, and I destroyed them from before you. 9 Then Balak the son of Zippor, king of Moab, arose to make war against Israel, and sent and called Balaam the son of Beor to curse you. 10 But I would not listen to Balaam; therefore he continued to bless you. So I delivered you out of his hand. 11 Then you went over the Jordan and came to Jericho. And the men of Jericho fought against you—*also* the Amorites, the Perizzites, the Canaanites, the Hittites, the Girgashites, the Hivites, and the Jebusites. But I delivered them into your hand. 12 I sent the hornet before you which drove them out from before you, *also* the two kings of the Amorites, *but* not with your sword or with your bow. 13 I have given you a land for which you did not labor, and cities which you did not build, and you dwell in them; you eat of the vineyards and olive groves which you did not plant.' 14 "Now therefore, fear the Lord, serve Him in sincerity and in truth, and put away the gods which your fathers served on the other side of the

River and in Egypt. Serve the Lord! 15 And if it seems evil to you to serve the Lord, choose for yourselves this day whom you will serve, whether the gods which your fathers served that *were* on the other side of the River, or the gods of the Amorites, in whose land you dwell. But as for me and my house, we will serve the Lord." 16 So the people answered and said: "Far be it from us that we should forsake the Lord to serve other gods; 17 for the Lord our God *is* He who brought us and our fathers up out of the land of Egypt, from the house of bondage, who did those great signs in our sight, and preserved us in all the way that we went and among all the people through whom we passed. 18 And the Lord drove out from before us all the people, including the Amorites who dwelt in the land. We also will serve the Lord, for He *is* our God." 19 But Joshua said to the people, "You cannot serve the Lord, for He *is* a holy God. He *is* a jealous God; He will not forgive your transgressions nor your sins. 20 If you forsake the Lord and serve foreign gods, then He will turn and do you harm and consume you, after He has done you good." 21 And the people said to Joshua, "No, but we will serve the Lord!" 22 So Joshua said to the people, "You *are* witnesses against yourselves that you have chosen the Lord for yourselves, to serve Him." And they said, "*We are* witnesses!" 23 "Now therefore," *he said,* "put away the foreign gods which *are* among you, and incline your heart to the Lord God of Israel." 24 And the people said to Joshua, "The Lord our God we will serve, and His voice we will obey!" 25 So Joshua made a covenant with the people that day, and made for them a statute and an ordinance in Shechem.

Joshua's Concern

Gathered at Shechem (v. 1), Joshua commenced to speak to the nation regarding God's faithfulness in the past (vv. 2–13). The reason he did this was to initiate a covenant renewal process, at the conclusion of which the people would make a vow to continue to follow God after Joshua's departure (vv. 16–17, 21, 25). The structure of Joshua's message resembles covenant treaties used in the Ancient Near East, such as suzerainty treaties between a lord and a vassal.[14] By delivering his message in this manner, Joshua was calling his brethren to account for God's work in their midst and challenging them to obedience as an expression of gratitude.

From an apologetic perspective, the message Joshua delivered was a type of preaching for discipleship, whereby the followers of God were given reasons to remain faithful. For Joshua, this concern would have been a matter of his legacy since Israel's future after his departure was anything but certain from the human perspective. While God's faithfulness was never in doubt, the experience of Israel under Joshua's leadership and before was marked by times of disobedience and failure, such as the sin of Achan and subsequent defeat at Ai (Josh 7). Sadly, the concerns about the generation after Joshua were realized in the repeated cycle of sin and judgment under the judges of Israel. Thus, Joshua's concern was to present a final message based on the evidence of God's faithfulness and the call to Israel to persevere.

Joshua's Apologetic Argument

Joshua's argument followed a cumulative approach of layering evidence upon evidence. He began with a reminder of God's deeds with Abraham (vv. 2–3), followed by a recounting of Jacob's descent into Egypt and Moses's leadership (vv. 4–5). He then rehearsed several instances of God's provision for Israel after delivering them from Pharaoh (vv. 6–10), including how Canaan was conquered (vv. 11–13). God's goodness, explained Joshua, provided Israel with "a land for which [they] did not labor, and cities which [they] did not build . . . [and] vineyards and olive groves which [they] did not plant" (v. 13).

At this point in his message, Joshua's approach changed from recalling God's blessings to challenging Israel to "fear the LORD, [to] serve Him in sincerity and in truth, and [to] put away the

---

14. Howard, *Joshua*, chap. 4, sect. 4, para. 2.

[false] gods [their] fathers served" (v. 14). He made his case based on God's acts, called the people to obedience and true worship, and then delivered what is probably the most memorable part of his message. "Choose for yourselves this day whom you will serve," Joshua demanded, followed by his declaration that "as for me and my house, we will serve the LORD" (v. 15).

Before examining the rationale for this demand and declaration by Joshua, recall that the purpose of his message was to establish the basis for Israel's renewal of their divinely-initiated covenant. Joshua presented an apologetic in favor of Israel continuing to live in obedience to God, an argument leading to a conclusion. Considered in the form of a syllogism, Joshua's argument may be conceived as follows:

P1: God has been faithful from Abraham to Joshua.

P2: God will always be faithful to Israel.

P3: A proper response to God's faithfulness is to serve him alone.

C: Therefore, Joshua will serve God, and so should Israel.

In this argument the abductive structure is discernible, as the evidence accumulates and leads to the inference that it is logical to choose to serve God. The argument is not deductive or inductive, as far as the premises are not undeniable, especially since some in Israel neither necessarily agreed that continuing to follow God was best, nor that he had always provided sufficiently. Though those who questioned God in this way were in disobedience, Joshua was not concerned to establish an unassailable proof to justify his actions. He carefully weighed the evidence and made his choice, inviting others to do the same.

Joshua's Invitation

Joshua gave his invitation to people to serve God in v. 15, and their answer was that they would not serve any God but the LORD (v. 16). After doing this, the people gave their own argument as to why they were making this choice, citing in a manner similar to

Joshua how God had provided (vv. 17–18). Then, in what R. D. Nelson describes as "a deep paradox," Joshua proceeded to tell the people that they were not able to do what they were committing to because God's holiness and jealousy would lead to their destruction in the event of disobedience (vv. 19–20).[15] As the people responded in protest and restated their promises of obedience to God, Joshua finally called them to witness against themselves in the event of future failings, concluding with a command that the people "put away the foreign gods which [were] among them, and incline [their] heart to the LORD God of Israel" (v. 23). The people responded that they would do so (v. 24), and the covenant was renewed (v. 25).

Aside from the enigmatic response and challenge from Joshua to the people's promises of obedience, this invitation reveals that Joshua was not going to force a conclusion upon his audience. He presented the evidence and left it to them to decide, and even his response to their decision shows his concern to carefully present the facts and expectations associated with his apologetic message. On a practical level, Joshua's example of moderation and refusal to accept what proved to be Israel's half-hearted response (cf. Judg 1:27—2:6) is a reminder to preachers. Presenting an argument and making an appeal need not involve coercion or any tolerance for what amounts to an emotional rush to judgment by the hearers. Make the case and an appeal based on the evidence, leaving time for reflection and decision. Urgency and passion are appropriate in apologetic preaching, but manipulation and hastiness are not.

Summary

This chapter presented a brief overview of types of argumentation used in apologetics: deductive, inductive, and abductive. Each type was defined and illustrated, and a rationale was offered for why I prefer abduction: it encourages epistemic humility in apologetic dialogue, and it helps avoid the error of oversimplification. Joshua

---

15. Nelson, *Joshua*, 276.

24:1–25 was also viewed through the lens of abductive apologetic argumentation, revealing that Joshua's concern is: to make a case for his belief; to argue abductively in making his case; and to invite his hearers to make a choice based on the evidence. The significance of these findings is general and specific. Generally, it is necessary for preachers to learn the basics of logical argumentation for the benefit of their preaching. When it comes to logic and arguments in apologetic preaching, the question is not *if* the preacher will use logic and make arguments, but *how* he will do so. Specifically, abduction was identified as a helpful approach to building a case for faith that is reasoned but not overly dogmatic. In the next chapter a model is presented to help preachers develop and deliver apologetic sermons for evangelism and discipleship.

CHAPTER 5

Preacher, Try This

The STEPS Model for Apologetic Preaching

In my estimation, this chapter is possibly the most significant for its usefulness in helping preachers begin to prepare and preach apologetic messages for evangelism and discipleship. The model presented to help preachers is my personal tool, developed over a sustained period of trial and error with apologetic preaching. Thus, what follows is a model for apologetic sermon structure, presented for both negative and positive apologetics. Though mentioned briefly in chapter 1, Nash's definition of negative and positive apologetics is helpful to remember in framing the discussion below:

> In negative apologetics, the major objective is producing answers to challenges to religious faith. The proper tack of negative apologetics is removing obstacles to belief... In negative apologetics, the apologist is playing defense. In positive apologetics, the apologist begins to play offense. It is one thing to show (or attempt to show) that assorted arguments against religious faith are weak or unsound; it is a rather different task to offer people

reasons why they should believe. The latter is the task of positive apologetics.[1]

Here, then, is the STEPS model of apologetic sermon structure. An example of the points in each model is provided within the context below, and summary outlines of the models are provided later in this chapter.

STEPS for Negative Apologetics

Specify the Apologetic Challenge

Given the concern in negative apologetics to defend the faith against attacks, the starting point in developing an apologetic sermon outline for negative apologetics is to specify the apologetic challenge the sermon intends to address. The preacher's goal at this point is to initiate a connection with the audience based on the topic under consideration. While there is not necessarily one "right" way to do this, it may prove useful to quote an opponent of the Christian faith, followed by a question. For example, to specify the apologetic challenge in response to the claims of an atheist that God does not exist, the preacher could begin as follows:

> If God exists, why is there so much evil in the world? A tsunami destroys several coastal villages, sweeping entire families into the sea. A military dictator decides a neighboring people are a threat and orders his troops to kill them all in a merciless genocidal purge. A car spins out of control on a patch of black ice, crashing into a ravine and leaving a mother and her infant son dead. These are real examples of evil in the world around us, and each one brings heartache and brokenness in its wake. Such struggles leave many unsure how to reconcile the existence of God and the existence of evil, and some even conclude that in a world of such pain God cannot exist.
>
> Maybe you agree with them and sit here today not believing in God, or at least you are not sure if God exists.

---

1. Nash, *Faith and Reason*, 14–15.

Pulpit Apologist

You have experienced evil and know of others who have, too, and now the idea of God seems more of a fairy tale than a reality. Surveys of religious beliefs, and specifically about whether God exists, show that you are not alone in your conclusion and questioning. Not everyone believes in God, and often the reason is related to the amount of evil in the world. Let's think about this together. Does evil in the world prove that God does not exist?

Tell the Critic's Best Argument

Having identified the apologetic challenge, the negative apologetic sermon now includes the best example of an argument in favor of the position stated in the challenge. It is important for the sake of integrity and fairness to the critic that whatever position is under consideration is presented accurately, without caricature. The preacher's goal at this point is to summarize the view of the opponent of Christianity in an understandable way and without making critical comments, at least not initially. Using the example of atheism related to evil, the preacher could do this as follows:

> Before I present what I think are good reasons to believe in the existence of God in spite of the evil in the world, I want to talk a bit more about what many atheists have argued in defense of the conclusion that evil rules out God's existence. The atheist begins by acknowledging the presence of evil in the world. Consider, for example, what I discussed earlier. The tsunami that kills thousands; a tyrant who commits genocide by killing an entire neighboring people; the mother and child who die in a car crash—these are examples of evil in world. The tsunami and car crash represent what may be called natural evil, and the genocide is an example of moral evil.
>
> If God exists, the atheist continues, then surely he would be powerful enough to stop evil, both natural and moral. God is all-powerful, right? Further, if God exists, then surely he would want to stop evil. God is all-good, right? Yet, evil still exists, both in natural disasters and in the wicked choices people make. So, the atheist

concludes that God is either not powerful enough to stop evil, or he is not really good, since he does not stop evil. Therefore, since evil exists, God must not exist, at least not an all-powerful and all-good God. This is especially challenging for the Christian conception of God, which considers God's power and goodness as essential to his existence. Thus, if the atheist is right, and evil proves God is not all-powerful or all-good, then what of the Christian God?[2]

Expose the Weakness of the Critic's Argument

The challenge and critic's argument have now been presented, so the preacher's task is to present in an accessible, non-complicated but substantive form the weaknesses in the critic's argument. The key at this point is to respond without leaving the impression that one must become an expert in atheism to answer an atheist. Further, the preacher must avoid sarcasm and oversimplification, remembering that the matters under discussion are connected to real people with genuine struggles who deserve more than trite, clichéd answers. For example, in dealing with evil and the existence of God, one could expose the weaknesses of the critic's argument in the following manner:

> But wait a minute. Before we conclude that the presence of evil in the world is proof that, if he exists, God is weak or not good, or that he maybe does not even exist, I think there are some problems with the atheist's argument. Let's consider these as questions. What if God is all-powerful and all-good, but he refuses to override human free will? While we can certainly imagine a world without moral evil—without genocidal military dictators, without child molesters, without rapists—such a world would also be somehow less than human if free will were taken away and the only reason for no moral evil was because there was no human freedom. True

---

2. For a similar argument, see Copan and Meister, *Philosophy of Religion*, 156–67.

freedom implies choices—the freedom to choose good and the freedom to choose evil.

Further, if God does not exist, then where does the atheist get the ideas of good and evil, of right and wrong? If the atheist responds that each person must decide what is right and wrong, then possibly what the rapist does is actually right in his own way of thinking. Even if the atheist refuses to go along with such relativism, insisting that there are actual moral facts, a real and objective right and wrong, they have no ultimate standard from which to make this conclusion. Moral laws require a moral lawgiver, but the atheist does not think one exists. There are other questions to ask the atheist who believes evil and God cannot coexist, but these represent what I think are the ones especially important for now.[3]

Present the Answer to the Apologetic Challenge

At this point the preacher will present what the Bible and other sources say about the apologetic challenge. The focus of the preacher turns from answering the critic to offering reasons to believe the Christian faith despite the apologetic challenge being discussed. When sharing the answer to the apologetic challenge, the preacher is helping the hearer understand that the Christian faith is both reasonable and based in divine revelation. When dealing with the atheist's claims regarding evil and the existence of God, the preacher could continue as follows:

> What does the Christian faith teach about God's existence, especially considering the presence of natural and moral evil in the world? For starters, the Bible explains that God made the world and everything and everyone in it, and that when he did this he made humans as his special representatives. Genesis 1:1 declares that "in the beginning God created the heavens and the earth," and in 1:27 that "God created man in His own image; in the image of God He created him; male and female He

---

3. See Copan and Meister, *Philosophy of Religion*, 127–39.

created them." However, as the Bible goes on to reveal, the first humans chose to disobey God in the very area we are discussing—in the area of good and evil. Genesis 2:15–17 describes how "the LORD God took the man and put him in the garden of Eden to tend and keep it. And the LORD God commanded the man, saying, 'Of every tree of the garden you may freely eat; but of the tree of the knowledge of good and evil you shall not eat, for in the day that you eat of it you shall surely die.'"

Perhaps you have heard how this all turned out—how the man and woman chose to disobey God and eat of the tree of the knowledge of good and evil, and how that resulted in several far-reaching consequences. These include a breakdown in human relationships and, eventually, the first murder. Likewise, the natural world became a difficult place for the man to work and live. What are we to make of this? It seems reasonable to me that the misuse of human freedom goes a long way in explaining the presence of evil in the world that God created. The account doesn't stop here, though. No, far from abandoning the world to evil, God began redeeming it, promising one day that he "will wipe away every tear . . . there shall be no more death, nor sorrow, nor crying. There shall be no more pain" (Rev 21:4). Thus, it also seems reasonable to me that God will one day bring an end to all evil and, though I am not immune from its effects, that God's existence is a key to understanding evil in the world.

Summarize and Transition to a Related Invitation

It is possible to present the first four parts of the STEPS model within a sermon that is broader than just the apologetics (e.g., a message about foolishness could include a discussion of the fool's denial of God's existence). However, if the message is wholly apologetic, then the preacher's last responsibility is to summarize and offer a gospel invitation relevant to the audience (i.e., if evangelism, then the gospel portion is an invitation to be saved, but if discipleship, then the gospel portion is an invitation to trust God more deeply; if both, then both). For example, in a message addressing evil and the existence of God, an evangelistic invitation could be as follows:

> I don't pretend that this brief message answers every question related to the presence of evil in the world and whether God exists. There are other aspects of the topic to discuss, and you may have even deeper, more personal questions. However, what we have heard does offer a possible solution to the dilemma created by evil. Yes, evil exists. There have been and will likely be more terrible natural disasters, more evil regimes, and more fatal crashes. Natural and moral evil are part of the world we live in, and they touch all of our lives. Does the Christian faith offer a solution? Absolutely, and it is not a simple, quick fix. The Christian faith not only offers an explanation for the presence of evil related to human freedom and the promise that evil will one day be fully dealt with; the Christian message is also one that includes God's own struggle with evil. Jesus Christ was the victim of moral evil. He was murdered in a most ruthless, painful manner, even though he had done no wrong. Jesus took evil personally, dying a criminal's death on a Roman cross, centuries ago. The Christian faith does not teach that it ended on the cross, though. Rather, as an example of how God will eventually overcome evil, Jesus rose from the dead and will return to earth someday.
>
> What does all this mean to you as you struggle with evil and God's existence? Maybe it means that you have begun to consider that evil is not all there is, that God really does exist. If that is you, I hope you will continue to wrestle with these matters and let the evidence build. Talk with the person who invited you here today or talk with me after the service. There is more to know about evil and God and the hope of the Christian message. Maybe you are that person here who has decided it is time to stop doubting and start believing. The evidence makes sense. You've heard this message and others like it, maybe even read books and talked with others, and now you are ready to follow the evidence where it leads. It

leads to Jesus, and in just a moment we will offer you an opportunity to talk with someone about taking the next step in your journey of faith.

Having considered how STEPS works in the case of a negative apologetic regarding the problem of evil and God's existence, here is an outline form offering another example. In this instance, STEPS is used in the case of a negative apologetic regarding the reliability of Scripture.

STEPS Example for Negative Apologetics: Outline Form

Can We Trust the Bible?

I. Specify the Apologetic Challenge

A. Critics say the Bible is full of errors.

B. Rather than a Holy Bible, they claim the Bible is full of holes.

C. So then, let's consider this challenge. Can we trust the Bible?

II. Tell the Critic's Best Argument

A. An example of challenges to the trustworthiness of the Bible found in the accounts of Judas's alleged death.

B. One account claims he hung himself, but another that he burst open after falling.

C. This is a contradiction, right?

III. Expose the Weakness of the Critic's Argument

A. Well, it could be a contradiction, but it could also be something else.

B. What the critic fails to consider is that the two accounts of Judas's death can be reconciled easily.

C. Just like when two people stand on either side of a street and report what happened in a car crash, each giving a unique perspective, so there are two perspectives on what happened to Judas.

IV. Present the Answer to the Apologetic Challenge

A. Rather than concluding that the Bible is full of errors, let's consider another possibility about Judas.

B. In the first instance, his manner of death is described. He hung himself. In the second instance, the consequences of his hanging are described. After his death, his body eventually fell to the ground, bursting open when it did.

C. We want to remember that the Bible is "inspired by God" (2 Tim 3:16), which means that God is its author. God cannot lie, and he cannot say contradictory things. God always speaks the truth. The Bible can be trusted.

V. Summarize and Transition to a Related Invitation

A. If you are a Christian and struggling with your confidence in the Bible, don't be afraid to ask questions. The answers are available to those who seek.

B. Maybe you are like the critic, not even sure about God and certainly not sure about the Bible. There are answers for you, too, if you are willing to seek.

C. As we stand to sing, won't you come and talk with me or one of the counselors? Whatever your need, whatever your doubts, whatever your questions, God has answers, and we will help you find them.

STEPS for Positive Apologetics

Specify the Apologetic Topic

In a positive apologetic message, where the goal is to present a positive case for belief, the preacher begins by specifying the apologetic topic. This approach sets the expectation with the hearer that the sermon will provide reasons to believe. It will help the preacher connect with his audience if, when introducing the apologetic topic, he avoids the language of doubt (though such language may prove helpful with negative apologetics), focusing instead on inviting the hearer into a deeper consideration of the positive case for believing. For example, if the resurrection of Jesus is the topic, then the preacher might begin as follows:

> What reasons are there to believe that Jesus rose from the dead? That question may surprise some of you, since you already believe Jesus rose, and you have never felt the need to develop a list of reasons for your belief. If that describes you, then I invite you to simply listen and consider why you believe what you believe. Remember, faith involves evidence and certainty, so what you hear today can be a help in growing your faith. Plus, you never know when the Lord is going to give you the opportunity to talk with someone who is not as sure as you about Jesus' resurrection, and you will be able to help them along after hearing this message.
>
> Maybe, though, you are new to the Christian faith and hunger to know more about your faith, or possibly someone has recently posed a question or objection about the resurrection that you would like to be able to answer with confidence. In either case, this message is for you, too. It's also offered with the seeker in mind, the one who is looking for answers and thinks Christianity may be where to find them. Whoever you are and whatever your situation, let's make a journey together and discover reasons to believe that Jesus rose from the dead.

Tell the Topic's Significance

After specifying the topic, the preacher gives the hearers a few key reasons why the topic is important. It will help the preacher to think in terms of doctrine and practice at this point. Help the listener understand the doctrinal significance of the topic, how it relates to overall Christian theology. Likewise, discuss how the topic generally relates to living the Christian life, to the practice of faith. In a message about Jesus' resurrection, the following could be preached:

> Before considering the biblical and rational basis for believing the resurrection occurred, consider a few of the theological and practical reasons the topic is significant. From a theological perspective the resurrection is an essential part of the gospel message. As Paul explains in 1 Corinthians 15:3-4, "I delivered to you first of all that which I also received: that Christ died for our sins according to the Scriptures, and that He was buried, and that He rose again the third day according to the Scriptures." In this passage we learn that the gospel is about Christ's death, burial, and resurrection—all three are fundamentals of the good news, but especially the resurrection. This is why Paul goes on in 15:14 and 17 to declare that "if Christ is not risen, then our preaching is empty and your faith is also empty . . . And if Christ is not risen, your faith is futile; you are still in your sins!" Clearly, the Christian faith depends upon the resurrection.
>
> Likewise, the resurrection is a practical help when considering our own mortality and the death of our loved ones who are Christians. Jesus' victory over death holds a promise of future things for all who believe, since every Christian, too, will one day rise from the dead if they die before Jesus returns. Paul's words in 1 Corinthians 15:20, 52, and 54 are especially helpful in this regard: "But now Christ is risen from the dead, and has become the firstfruits of those who have fallen asleep . . . For the trumpet will sound, and the dead will be raised incorruptible . . . So when this corruptible has put on incorruption, and this mortal put on immortality, then shall be brought to pass the saying that is written: 'Death is swallowed up in victory.'" What is the basis of this hope? The resurrection of Jesus from the dead! Death is not the final word. Resurrection is! Eternal joy is coming because Jesus rose from the dead.

Explain the Biblical and Rational Basis Concerning the Apologetic Topic

The topic has been presented and its significance considered, so the preacher turns to a presentation of the biblical and rational basis for believing whatever is under consideration. This is the central apologetic content of the message, where the argument in favor of the belief is put forth in clear and compelling terms. While the preacher's goal is not to harangue his hearers and browbeat them concerning the topic, he should make an impassioned case for "the hope that is in [him]" (1 Pet 3:15). In the case of the resurrection of Jesus, the preacher could proceed as follows:

> The biblical evidence for the resurrection of Jesus is plentiful. Paul testifies that Jesus "rose again the third day according to the Scriptures, and that He was seen by Cephas, then by the twelve. After that he was seen by over five hundred brethren at once . . . After that He was seen by James, then by all the apostles. Then last of all He was seen by me also" (1 Cor 15:4–7). Concerning the five hundred brethren Paul describes, he explains that "the greater part remain to the present, but some have fallen asleep" (1 Cor 15:6). Why is this significant? Only because Paul was making a public claim that many who saw Jesus after his resurrection were still alive at the time the letter to the Corinthians was written. Paul was appealing to eyewitness testimony writ large. Further, Matthew, Mark, Luke, and John all give accounts of the resurrection in their Gospel narratives, each providing specific details about when the empty tomb was discovered, who was there, as well as accounts of the encounters they and others had with Jesus after he arose. These examples indicate there is strong biblical evidence to support Jesus' resurrection from the dead.
>
> What about other reasons to believe the resurrection account? Consider the historical testimony of leaders in the early church after the time of the apostles. Men like Origen, Polycarp, and Justin Martyr—sometimes referred to as church fathers—all testify to the resurrection of Jesus as both historical fact and having pastoral

significance. Consider also the personal changes in the apostles after the resurrection—how Peter went from denying Jesus to boldly proclaiming him as the risen Lord, and how Paul went from persecutor of Christians to missionary for Jesus and defender of the resurrection. Finally, if the resurrection did not happen, then why didn't the Jewish authorities simply produce the body of Jesus and end the early church's growth and influence? They didn't do so because the body of Jesus was not in the tomb. He rose from the dead, just as he promised. This isn't all the biblical and rational evidence for the resurrection, but there is certainly much that is worthwhile in what we have considered. The evidence is in, and there is good reason to believe that Jesus rose from the dead.[4]

Practically Apply the Apologetic Topic for the Hearers

This is where the preacher transitions from apologetic case-making to practical application. How does the apologetic topic relate to the hearers? The emphasis at this point is in making apologetic realities fit real life needs. In the case of the resurrection, practical application could be as follows:

> Amid all this talk of biblical and rational evidence there are also particular practical benefits to the resurrection for each of your lives. Perhaps you are struggling with a sinful habit and you seem to always make one step forward but two steps back. As a Christian you can gain the victory because of the resurrection of Jesus. That's right! According to Romans 8:10–11, "If Christ is in you, the body is dead because of sin, but the Spirit is life because of righteousness. But if the Spirit of Him who raised Jesus from the dead dwells in you, He who raised Jesus from the dead will also give life to your mortal bodies through His Spirit who dwells in you." Without the resurrection you are powerless, but with the resurrection comes power through the Spirit. You can overcome sin in your life because Jesus rose from the dead.

4. See Geisler, *Christian Apologetics*, 405–16.

Another benefit to believing the resurrection happened relates to the brokenness in our world. Do you ever find yourself thinking that the news is always bad, that things just seem to get worse and worse? You are not alone, and the world is a dark place in many ways. However, because of the resurrection of Jesus there is hope that one day the world will be put to right. Concerning this hope, Paul's words in 1 Corinthians 15:22–25 are comforting: "For as in Adam all die, even so in Christ all shall be made alive. But each one in his own order: Christ the firstfruits, afterward those who are Christ's at His coming. Then comes the end, when He delivers the kingdom to God the Father, when He puts an end to all rule and all authority and power. For He must reign till He has put all enemies under His feet. The last enemy that will be destroyed is death." These verses remind us that the resurrection of Jesus is more than a doctrine, more than a historical fact—it is the final hope for an end to suffering and the beginning of a better world.

Summarize and Transition to a Related Invitation

As with the STEPS model applied to negative apologetics, so it is possible for the positive model to be a part of a message dealing with something not exclusively apologetic. If so, there is not necessarily a transition to a related invitation. However, if the positive apologetic message is stand-alone, then the preacher will conclude by summarizing and making a transition appropriate to the topic and audience—unbeliever, believer, or both. In a message about the resurrection of Jesus the invitation could be as follows:

> We started by asking about the reasons to believe that Jesus rose from the dead. We have considered this question in several ways, including its theological and practical importance, the biblical and rational case for believing in the resurrection, and how the resurrection matters in particular circumstances of our lives. I trust that you feel the weight of the evidence concerning Jesus' resurrection, and that your faith is strengthened. If you are

seeking answers, I pray you give sincere consideration to those offered here.

As we conclude I would like to give this simple invitation. Christian, the resurrection is central to your faith. Perhaps it is time to give yourself to serious study of its reliability, asking God to give you opportunities to share the evidence for the resurrection with others. Will you do that today? Someone in your life needs to hear about the resurrection, and you are the one to tell them. What about you, the seeker who came today looking for answers? As I just stated, I pray you give sincere consideration to those answers offered here. Jesus died for you, and was buried and rose again, all for you. He offers to give you new life, resurrection life. Will you accept his offer today?

Having considered how STEPS works in the case of a positive apologetic regarding the resurrection of Jesus, here is an outline form offering another example. In this instance, STEPS is used in the case of a positive apologetic regarding the reliability of Scripture.

STEPS Example for Positive Apologetics: Outline Form

Why We Can Trust the Bible

I. Specify the Apologetic Topic

A. The Bible is God's revelation to us, our standard and guide.

B. As Christians, we need to know that we can trust the Bible

C. So then, let's consider why we can trust the Bible.

II. Tell the Topic's Significance

A. It important for us to trust the Bible because it teaches us what we should believe.

B. It also teaches us how we should live.

C. A Christian's confidence in the Bible will ultimately reflect in his confidence in God.

III. Explain the Biblical and Rational Basis Concerning the Topic

A. Why can we trust the Bible? Consider two reasons.

B. First, the Bible tells us that God is its source, and we know that God cannot lie, and he cannot say contradictory things. God always speaks the truth. The Bible can be trusted.

C. Second, when it comes to evidence both inside its pages and in the history of its existence, the Bible has more than enough evidence to allow it to stand up under scrutiny in a court of law. The Bible has more evidence for its accuracy than there is evidence that George Washington ever lived.

IV. Practically Apply the Apologetic Topic for the Hearers

A. Knowing the Bible is true means you can trust its promises. You can count on God.

B. Knowing the Bible is true means you can trust its history. The events in the Bible happened.

C. Knowing the Bible is true means you can trust its Savior. Jesus really died for our sins and rose the third day, and he will come again someday.

V. Summarize and Transition to a Related Invitation

A. Christian, take comfort. Your Bible is trustworthy.

B. If you are not a Christian, the Bible still has something to say to you. God loves you and wants a relationship with you. Jesus died for your sins and offers you forgiveness and a new life.

C. As we stand to sing, won't you come and talk with me or one of the counselors? Whatever your need, whatever your concerns, whatever your questions, God has answers, and we will help you find them.

Summary

In this chapter I provided an overview of the STEPS model for delivering negative and positive apologetic sermons. To recap, the negative STEPS model is:

- Specify the apologetic challenge.
- Tell the critic's best argument.
- Expose the weakness of the critic's argument.
- Present the biblical answer to the apologetic challenge.
- Summarize and transition to a related invitation.

The positive STEPS model is:

- Specify the apologetic topic.
- Tell the topic's significance.
- Explain the biblical and rational basis for believing the apologetic topic.
- Practically apply the apologetic topic for the hearers.
- Summarize and transition to a related invitation.

My intention in presenting the STEPS model in this chapter was to bring a practical application to the discussion of apologetic preaching so that those who may agree with the importance of the topic also have a means to apply it in the pulpit.

Conclusion
A Plea for Apologetic Preaching

Before we conclude our exploration, I want to quickly summarize a few of the implications of the discussion thus far, as well as put into a few simple sentences the basic argument I have attempted. Finally, I want to make one final plea for apologetic preaching.

So What?

It is fair to ask an author, "So what?" when it comes to the outcome of his or her work. Thus, let's take a moment to develop a few of the implications—the "So what?"—regarding our discussion about preaching and apologetics in the preceding chapters. For example, preaching and apologetics are important means to aid in the church's mission to reach the world with the gospel. As unbelief and secularism continue to rise, along with philosophical and religious pluralism, the concomitance of preaching and apologetics is arguably as important as it was in the time of the apostles. Apologetic preaching for evangelism offers a viable and adaptive means to engage the skeptic and seeker in a substantive and reasoned manner. Likewise, apologetic preaching for discipleship offers pastors a way to help Christians with different types of doubt and to prepare them to effectively interact with those of other worldviews.

Conclusion

Furthermore, as a supplement to the numerous resources available concerning apologetics and regarding the importance of preaching, I hope this work adds a theoretical and practical dimension to the discussion of how they relate. Theoretically, the rationale for and distinctives of apologetic preaching discussed in the preceding chapters offer pastors a justification for apologetic preaching. Practically, the STEPS model helps those looking for a method of apologetic preaching and may inspire others to develop their own methods. Given the expectations placed on pastors to be both intellectual and practical in their ministry, and the centrality of preaching in pastoral ministry, there is a benefit to understanding and applying the conclusions of our investigation.

Finally, the study of differing forms of argumentation in apologetic preaching may point to part of the difficulty in seeing congregations embrace apologetics as part of their ongoing life together and in their evangelistic efforts for reaching the world around them. If every apologetic argument has to meet the standard of deduction or induction, then very few, if any, will be able to perform the task. However, an apologetic case that builds cumulatively, is argued abductively, and points toward the veracity of the Christian worldview is something that pastors can present in their sermons. Yet, it is possible that few pastors have any awareness of the nuances of argumentation and how they relate to apologetics and preaching—and perhaps upon reading this material they will find help for themselves in these areas.

More Needs to be Said

No doubt, this is not the final or even best word about preaching and apologetics. Other areas of exploration may prove helpful, such as the following. Concerning approaches to apologetics methodology, are there certain methods that are more biblical than others? For example, is it correct of Groothuis to interpret Paul's basic approach as classical, or was Paul an evidentialist?[1]

---

1. Groothuis, *Christian Apologetics*, chap. 2.

Conclusion

What about method and apologetic preaching? Is there an apologetic method that best suits evangelistic preaching? Discipleship preaching? What about existential arguments for the existence of God, or fideistic approaches? Is the Bible concerned with such things, or is this an area of freedom for the preacher integrating apologetics into his sermons? Further research relative to these questions would touch on the topic of the mechanics of apologetics and preaching from the theoretical perspective.

Concerning abduction in apologetic preaching, are there biblical examples beyond Joshua 24? To consider an even more fundamental question: Does the Bible intend to address the matter of logical argumentation? While I focused on abduction, is it possible that this is an example of anachronistic reading of the text? I don't think it is, but it is a fair question if the matter of argumentation is to be given a central consideration in the broader topic of apologetic preaching. Another related question is whether there is a continuum of argumentation, such that to address one type of audience (e.g., the prophets of Baal) requires one type of argumentation, but when addressing another audience (e.g., the Athenians) the preacher should adopt a different type of argumentation. Matters of this type go beyond apologetic methodology to an exploration of the specific ways in which methodology is applied.

Concerning biblical examples of apologetic preaching, what about a biblical survey of apologetic preaching? While the examples of Paul in Athens, Jude, and Joshua were considered, their selection was based on types of apologetic preaching. Yet, if one were to conduct a study of every instance of addressing unbelievers in Scripture, or of messages directed to believers, would there be any themes of apologetics that emerge? The value of such inquiry is the ability to gain a panoramic view of how apologetics relates to the metanarrative of Scripture, especially based upon God's intention to see the world saved. Is there a concomitant relationship between God's plan of redemption and apologetics in the Bible, and how could it relate to preaching?

Concerning apologetics and homiletics training, a further area of inquiry is the role that apologetics plays in teaching preaching. Is there a consensus among homiletics professors about the value of apologetics in preaching, and are courses available in this area? Sadly, my experience in seminary at an evangelical institution did not include any training in apologetics during an entire Master of Divinity curriculum. Even in advanced studies for a Master of Theology, including coursework in homiletics, not once did apologetics and preaching appear in the reading or assignments. Is this a typical experience, and what, if any, are the plans to address concerns about the need for apologetics in preaching amid the post-modern milieu in the United States and elsewhere? It seems to me that this concern hints at the possibility that there is a gap in ministerial formation when it comes to apologetics and preaching.

Finally, concerning pastoral care, an exploration of how apologetics might enhance counseling and other areas of ministry is possibly an additional area of study. In my own practice of pastoral counseling there are instances when apologetics aids in answering a counselee's doubt or other concern. However, sometimes the need in counseling is less rationally derived and more affective. Is there a place for apologetics in such instances? If a couple is grieving a stillborn child, part of the counseling need may touch on rational components of the problem of evil and the justice of God, and apologetics could serve the counseling process in this way. Yet, there are also emotional needs in such instances, and a standard apologetic argument may have little positive effect. This raises the matter of how the pastor knows when apologetics does and does not serve the counseling process. Other applications of apologetics to pastoral care are possible, as well. Is it fitting for a minister conducting a funeral service to defend the resurrection in his graveside remarks? Should a wedding exhortation include content touching on the biblical view of marriage? When making a hospital visit should the pastor prepare for evangelistic opportunities with family members based on an apologetic for the goodness of God? As with the concern about possible gaps in ministerial preparation relating to apologetics and preaching, so there may also be a need to give pastors a rationale for and practical means of integrating apologetics into ministry outside of the pulpit.

Theses Regarding Preaching and Apologetics

As promised, here are a few sentences to summarize the gist of my argument regarding the importance of bringing together preaching and apologetics.

1. Preaching in a post-modern, relativistic milieu reveals that apologetics will be needed to effectively reach seekers and skeptics.
2. Preaching in a church significantly affected by the post-modern, relativistic milieu also reveals the need to effectively disciple Christians who come to faith in such a context.
3. Thus, apologetics is important to consider for preaching as evangelism and preaching as discipleship.
4. The biblical witness provides examples of such apologetic preaching for evangelism and discipleship.
5. Apologetic preaching is, therefore, rooted in biblical examples and teaching, and faithfulness to Scripture requires that preachers take seriously the need to engage in apologetic preaching for evangelism and discipleship.

Preacher, Make an Apology!

John and Sheila, the individuals we met in the opening paragraphs of the introduction, both heard and benefitted from preaching that included apologetics. In John's situation, his faith was strengthened by his pastor's messages. He learned reasons to believe, and his doubts were answered. In Sheila's circumstances, she found answers to questions about God and began to explore further. She is seeking, and apologetic preaching helped her along the way. Every community of believers has someone like John, and every person

Conclusion

probably knows a seeker like Sheila. How to reach them is the concern, and apologetic preaching provides pastors a way to address that concern. Evangelistic preaching that is infused with passional reason and strong apologetic content is a powerful weapon in the preacher's arsenal and a key to victory in the winning of souls. Likewise, discipleship preaching utilizing biblical and rational arguments to defend and explain the hope of the gospel is an important part of the shepherd's calling in tending and feeding the flock entrusted to him by the Good Shepherd. The obedient preacher will heed Paul's admonition to "preach the word! Be ready in season and out of season. Convince, rebuke, exhort, with all longsuffering and teaching" (2 Tim 4:2), and the wisest preacher will do so incorporating apologetics. Whether for evangelism or discipleship, apologetics and preaching belong together. Preacher, make an apology!

Bibliography

Anderson, Ray S. *An Emergent Theology for Emerging Churches.* Downers Grove: InterVarsity, 2006.
Baggett, David, and Jerry L. Walls. *God and Cosmos: Moral Truth and Human Meaning.* Oxford: Oxford University Press, 2016. Kindle.
———. *Good God: The Theistic Foundations of Morality.* Oxford: Oxford University Press, 2011.
Baggett, David, and Marybeth Baggett. *The Morals of the Story: Good News about a Good God.* Downers Grove: InterVarsity, 2018.
Bock, Darrel L. "Acts." In *Holman Apologetics Commentary on the Bible: The Gospels and Acts.* Nashville: Broadman and Holman, 2013. Kindle.
Calvin, John. "Jude." In *Commentaries on the Catholic Epistles.* Translated by John Owen. https://www.ccel.org/ccel/calvin/calcom45.viii.ii.viii.html.
Carson, D. A. *Becoming Conversant with the Emerging Church: Understanding a Movement and Its Implications.* Grand Rapids: Zondervan, 2005.
———. *The Gagging of God: Christianity Confronts Pluralism.* Grand Rapids: Zondervan, 2011.
Chapell, Brian. *Christ-Centered Preaching: Redeeming the Expository Sermon.* Grand Rapids: Baker, 2018.
Chatraw, Joshua D., and Mark D. Allen. *Apologetics at the Cross: An Introduction for Christian Witness.* Grand Rapids: Zondervan, 2018.
Copan, Paul, and Chad Meister, eds. *Philosophy of Religion.* Oxford: Wiley & Sons, 2008.
Copan, Paul, and William Lane Craig, eds. *Contending with Christianity's Critics.* Nashville: B&H Academic, 2009.
Craig, William Lane. *Reasonable Faith: Christian Truth and Apologetics.* Wheaton: Crossway, 2008.
Craig, William Lane, and Chad Meister, eds. *God is Great, God is Good: Why Believing in God is Reasonable and Responsible.* Grand Rapids: InterVarsity, 2009.
Dawkins, Richard. *The God Delusion.* New York: Houghton Mifflin, 2008.
Dorman, Ted M. *A Faith for All Seasons.* 2nd ed. Nashville: Broadman and Holman, 2001.

Bibliography

Doskocil, Brad. "Jude." In *Grace New Testament Commentary: 1–2 Peter and Jude*. Denton, TX: Grace Evangelical Society, 2013. Kindle.

Elwell, Walter A., ed. *Evangelical Dictionary of Theology*. 2nd ed. Grand Rapids: Baker, 2001.

Erickson, Millard J. *Truth or Consequences: The Promise and Perils of Postmodernism*. Downers Grove: InterVarsity, 2001.

Fabarez, Michael. *Preaching That Changes Lives*. Eugene: Wipf & Stock, 2005.

Geisler, Norman L. *Christian Apologetics*. 2nd ed. Grand Rapids: Baker Academic, 2013.

———. *Systematic Theology*. Minneapolis: Bethany House, 2011.

Gentry, Thomas J. "Knowing the Savior: A Critical Assessment of Philosophical Religious Pluralism, Christian Pluralism, and Christian Inclusivism." *Aletheias* 3 (Spring 2018) 45–72. https://www.piedmontu.edu/file/aletheias---grad-journal/4.12.18-Final-Aletheias.pdf.

———. "Unleashing Faith by Bearing One Another's Burdens: An Exploration of the Biblical Rationale for and Practice of Christians Helping Christians through Lay Counseling Ministries." *Aletheias* (Spring 2017). https://www.piedmontu.edu/file/aletheias---grad-journal/3.29.17-Aletheias.pdf.

———. *You Shall Be My Witnesses: Reflections on Sharing the Gospel*. Charleston: CreateSpace, 2018. Kindle.

Gibbs, Eddie, and Ryan K. Bolger. *Emerging Churches: Creating Christian Community in Postmodern Cultures*. Grand Rapids: Baker Academic, 2005.

Groothuis, Douglas. *Christian Apologetics: A Comprehensive Case for Biblical Faith*. Downers Grove: InterVarsity, 2011. Kindle.

Gundry, Stanley N., and Steven B. Cowan, eds. *Five Views on Apologetics*. Grand Rapids: Zondervan, 2000.

Habermas, Gary. *Dealing with Doubt*. Chicago: Moody, 1990.

Harris, Sam. *Letters to a Christian Nation*. New York: Knopf, 2006.

Hitchens, Christopher. *God is not Great: How Religion Poisons Everything*. New York: Twelve, 2007.

Howard, David M., Jr. *Joshua*. The New American Commentary 5. Nashville: Broadman & Holman, 1998. Kindle.

Howell, Don N. *Servants of the Servant: A Biblical Theology of Leadership*. Eugene, OR: Wipf & Stock, 2003.

Hunter, George G., III. *The Celtic Way of Evangelism: How Christianity Can Reach the West Again*. Nashville: Abingdon, 2010.

Johnson, Darrell W. *The Glory of Preaching: Participating in God's Transformation of the World*. Downers Grove: IVP Academic, 2009.

Keller, Timothy. *Preaching: Communicating Faith in an Age of Skepticism*. New York: Penguin, 2016. Kindle.

Lewis, C. S. *Mere Christianity*. 1952. Reprint, London: Fount, 1997.

Lewis, Gordon R., and Bruce A. Demarest. *Integrative Theology*. Grand Rapids: Zondervan, 1996.

Bibliography

Loscalzo, Craig A. *Apologetic Preaching: Proclaiming Christ to a Postmodern World*. Downers Grove: InterVarsity, 2000.
Luther, Martin. "Controlling Your Thoughts." In *Faith Alone: A Daily Devotional*, edited by James C. Galvin. 1546. Reprint, Grand Rapids: Zondervan, 2005.
Markos, Louis. *Apologetics for the 21st Century*. Wheaton: Crossway, 2010.
Martyr, Justin. "Dialogue with Trypho." In *Ante-Nicene Fathers* 1. New York: Christian Literature, 1885.
McDill, Wayne. *12 Essential Skills for Great Preaching*. 2nd ed. Nashville: Broadman & Holman, 2006. Kindle.
McDowell, Sean, ed. *A New Kind of Apologist: Adopting Fresh Strategies, Addressing the Latest Issues, Engaging the Culture*. Eugene, OR: Harvest House, 2016.
McLaren, Brian D. *A New Kind of Christian*. San Francisco: Jossey-Bass, 2001.
―――. *A New Kind of Christianity*. New York: HarperCollins, 2010.
Nash, Ronald. *Faith and Reason*. Grand Rapids: Zondervan, 1988.
Nelson, Richard D. *Joshua: A Commentary*. The Old Testament Library. Louisville: Westminster John Knox, 1997.
Oden, Thomas C. *Ministry through Word and Sacrament*. Classical Pastoral Care 2. Grand Rapids: Baker Academic, 1987.
Parsons, Mikeal C. *Acts*. Paideia: Commentaries on the New Testament. Grand Rapids: Baker Academic, 2008. Kindle.
Pascal, Blaise. *Pensees*. Translated by W. F. Trotter. 1657. Reprint, London: GlobalGrey, 2017. Kindle.
Polhill, John B. *Acts*. The New American Commentary 26. Nashville: Broadman & Holman, 1992.
"Resurrection Did Not Happen, Say Quarter of Christians." BBC News. https://www.bbc.com/news/uk-england-39153121.
Richard, Ramesh. *Preparing Evangelistic Sermons: A Seven-step Method for Preaching Salvation*. 2nd ed. Grand Rapids: Baker, 2015.
Robinson, Haddon W. *Biblical Preaching: The Development and Delivery of Expository Messages*. Grand Rapids: Baker, 2014. Kindle.
Schreiner, Thomas R. *1, 2 Peter, Jude*. The New American Commentary 37. Nashville: Broadman & Holman, 2003.
Sire, James W. *The Universe Next Door*. 5th ed. Downers Grove: InterVarsity, 2009.
Smither, Edward L. *Augustine as Mentor: A Model for Preparing Spiritual Leaders*. Nashville: Broadman & Holman, 2008.
Stalker, James. *The Preacher and His Models*. Yale Lectures on Preaching, 1891. London: Hodder and Stoughton, 2008.
Streett, R. Alan. *The Effective Invitation*. Grand Rapids: Kregel, 2004.
Taylor, Charles. *A Secular Age*. Cambridge, MA: Belknap, 2007.
Taylor, Douglas E. "One from the Beginning: A Proposed Apologetic for the Growth of the Church from AD 30–250." PhD diss., Liberty University, 2018.

Vibert, Simon. *Excellence in Preaching: Studying the Craft of Leading Preachers.* Downers Grove: InterVarsity, 2011.

Wainwright, William J. *Reason and the Heart: A Prolegomenon to a Critique of Passional Reason.* Ithaca: Cornell University Press, 1995.

Watson, Duane F. *Invention, Arrangement and Style: Rhetorical Criticism of Jude and 2 Peter.* Atlanta: Scholars, 1988.

White, James E. *Meet Generation Z: Understanding and Reaching the New Post-Christian World.* Grand Rapids: Baker, 2017.

Wilkens, Steve, and Mark L. Sanford. *Hidden Worldviews: Eight Cultural Stories That Shape Our Lives.* Downers Grove: IVP Academic, 2009.

Wilkins, Michael J. *Matthew.* NIV Application Commentary: New Testament 1. Grand Rapids: Zondervan, 2009.

Williams, Clifford. *Existential Reasons for Belief in God: A Defense of Desires and Emotions for Faith.* Downers Grove: IVP Academic, 2011.

Witherington, Ben, III. "Jude: Another Brother's Sermon." In *Letters and Homilies for Jewish Christians.* Downers Grove: InterVarsity, 2007.

Zacharias, Ravi, and Norman Geisler, eds. *Is Your Church Ready? Motivating Leaders to Live an Apologetic Life.* Grand Rapids: Zondervan, 2003.

Zodhiates, Spiros, ed. *The Complete Word Study Dictionary: New Testament.* Chattanooga: AMG, 1992.

———. *The Complete Word Study New Testament.* Chattanooga: AMG, 1992.

Index

abduction
    advantages of, 42–43
    as apologetic preaching in Joshua, 37–42
    building a case for faith, 43
    defined in logical discourse, xx
    example arguing for God's existence, 33–34
    examples in apologetic preaching beyond Joshua 24, 63
    keeping the apologist in check, 35
abductive argumentation, 31, 33–37
abductive structure, of Joshua's argument, 41
Acts 17:16–32, apologetic preaching in, 7–12
affective moral elements, 30
antagonism, examples of, xiin10
apocryphal books/accounts, Jude's references to, 20–21
apologetic argumentation
    of Joshua, 40–41
    of Jude, 20–21
    in rational argumentation, 31
    taking time and patience, 37
apologetic case, building cumulatively, 62
apologetic challenge
    in negative apologetics, 45–46, 48–49
    in regard to the Bible, 51, 52
    in response to the claims of an atheist, 45–46
apologetic content, in preaching, xii, xiv
apologetic dialogue, epistemic humility in, 34–35
apologetic evangelistic preaching, 7n11, 12
apologetic excurses, taking necessary, 16n8
apologetic methodology, 10, 62–65
apologetic preaching. See also preaching
    abductive argumentation in, 31
    engaging the skeptic and seeker, 61
    as evangelism, 1–12
    logic and arguments in, 43
    making arguments and, 31–43
    plea for, 61–66
    practical application of, 60
    rooted in biblical examples and teaching, 65
    STEPS model for, 44–60
    taking time, 36
apologetic preaching as discipleship
    addressing doubts and challenges to the faith, 14

Index

apologetic preaching as discipleship *(continued)*
  aiding in guarding the flock, 16–17
  extremes of, 22
  in Jude, 17–23
  providing unique opportunities, 23
apologetic sermon structure, STEPS model of, 45
apologetic topic
  applying practically, 59
  explaining biblical and rational basis, 55–56
  practically applying, 56–57
  specifying, 52–53, 58
apologetics
  applications to pastoral care, xviin19, 64
  being balanced in, 28
  as the calling of all believers, xxi, 20
  conducted with unbelievers and believers, xix
  considering for preaching, 65
  defined, xix
  equipping questioning or doubting Christian to find intellectual confidence, 13
  explaining faith, xxi
  goal to honor God and his word, xxi
  as a handmaiden to the pulpit, xv
  integrating into ministry outside of the pulpit, 65
  integrating into preaching, xii
  Nash's definition of negative and positive, 44–45
  needed to reach seekers and skeptics, 65
  as primarily cerebral and rational, 27–28
  purpose of, 28
  reducing to assertions without arguments, 31
  relating to the metanarrative of Scripture, 63
  removing obstacles to repentance and faith, xxi
  role in teaching preaching, 63–64
  setting a tone in the congregation from the pulpit, 16
  teaching the "how" of, 15–16
Apologetics at the Cross (Chatraw and Allen), xixn24
apologia, as the basis for the English word "apologetics," xiii
apologists, 27, 35
apostles, changes in after the resurrection, 56
Applying, to specific life instances as part of COACH, 26n4
argumentation
  continuum of, 63
  deductive and inductive, 32–33
  differing forms of in apologetic preaching, 62
  in Revelation, xiiin12–xivn12
assumptions, of the author, xx–xxi
audience
  initiating connection with, 45
  Jews as the primary in the early church, 5
  Joshua not forcing a conclusion on his, 42
  metanarrative reaching a postmodern, 6n10
  of the pastor, xi
  Paul's appeal to, 11–12
Augustine, 15
author, assumptions of, xx–xxi
awe, 30

Baggett, David, and Marybeth Baggett, 34
Baird, John, xixn23

Index

balanced apologetics, engaging the whole person, 28
baseline cultural narratives, applying the gospel to, 2
Becoming Conversant with the Emerging Church (Carson), xivn13
being present with those we love, 30
belief, 35
believers
  in Acts, 4
  apologetics as the calling of all, xxi, 20
  apologetics conducted with, xix
  Calvin's comment on Jude's exhortation to, 22
  care of others and selfcare of, 22
  commanded to be ready to give a defense, xiii
  helping overcome doubt, 13
  instructing in their shared faith, 19
  Jude looking to help shore up, 22
  overcoming doubt, xvi
  presenting Scripture to, xix
  proclamation of God's message to, xviii
Bible
  as the inerrant and infallible Word of God, xxi
  as inspired by God, 52
  not contradicting itself, xxi
  trusting, 51–52, 58, 59
biblical and rational basis, 55, 59
biblical evidence, supporting Jesus' resurrection, 55
biblical examples, of apologetic preaching, 63
biblical orthodoxy, maintaining, 16
biblical witness, providing examples of apologetic preaching, 65

Bock, Darrel L., 9–10

Calvin, John, 22
care of others, by believers, 22
caricature, 27
certainty, associated with argumentation, 35
Chapell, Brian, xviiin21
Chesterton, G. K., 6
Christ-Centered Preaching (Chapell), xviiin21
Christian Apologetics (Groothuis), 13n1, 31n1
Christian community
  in Acts, 4, 4n6
  knowing and doing the will of God, 13
Christian faith. *See* faith
Christian growth, removing obstacles to, 14–17
Christian message, in the early church, 4
Christian worldview, x, 2, 36
Christians
  discipling in the post-modern, relativistic milieu, 65
  engaging in apologetics when appropriate, xiii
  keeping doubt from minds and hearts, 14
Chronicles of Narnia (Lewis), 6
claims, of absolute certainty, 35
classical apologetics, 10
COACH acrostic, terms in, 26n4
common ground, Paul's use of, 9–10
communication, of the gospel message, 5–6
community. *See* Christian community
concern, of Joshua, 39–40, 43
congregation
  Jude's reminders to, 22–23
  maintaining limits of orthodoxy within, 16

Index

Connecting, as part of COACH, 26n4
connection
  between apologetics and preaching, x
  with the audience, 45
content, conveying the gospel, 5
conversion, taking time, 36
cosmic security, need for, 29–30
counseling, apologetics enhancing, 64
covenant renewal process, Joshua initiating, 39
covenant treaties, in the Ancient Near East, 40
Craig, William Lane, 32
Craig's argument, for God's existence, 35–36
Creator, God as, 10
credibility, of a worldview, 36
critic's best argument
  exposing the weakness of, 47–48, 51–52
  telling in a negative apologetic sermon, 46–47
Cultivating, "I can't" tension as part of COACH, 26n4
culture, Paul's awareness of, 9, 10–11
cumulative case abductive argument, xxii
cumulative presentation, building faith, 36

Dawkins, Richard, xvi
Dealing with Doubt (Habermas), 13n1
death, 54
deduction, xx, 32, 33
deed, as a vital corollary to word, 5
defense, from the Greek word *apologia*, xiii
definitions, key, xviii–xx
Dennett, Daniel, xvi
discipleship preaching, 61
  defined, xix, 13
  overcoming doubt, xvi–xvii
  utilizing biblical and rational arguments, 66
distinctives, of apologetic preaching, 1–2, 14
divine (*sensus divinitatis*), human sense of, 10
doctrinal significance, 17, 53
Doskicil, Brad, 19–20
doubt
  avoiding the language of, 53
  coming at Christians, 14
  God answering, 52
  identifying the type of, 13n1
  overcoming, xvi–xvii, 13
  sources of, 14
doubting Christians, challenges posed by, xiv
doxology, Jude's concluding, 21n16

early church, 4–5, 17, 55–56
The Effective Invitation (Streett), 12n18
Emergent Church movement, xivn13
An Emergent Theology (Anderson), xivn13
Emerging Churches (Gibbs and Bolger), xivn13
Epicurean and Stoic phiolosophers, on Mars Hill, 9
epistemic humility, in apologetic dialogue, 34–35
eternal significance, of false teaching, 21
evangelism
  apologetic preaching and, 1–12, 61
  apologetics increasing pastoral confidence, xvii
  difference between process and moment in, 36n11

evangelistic implications, of a message designed for discipleship, xn1
evangelistic invitation, 50–51
evangelistic preaching. *See also* preaching
　centering on sin, righteousness, and redemption, 26–27
　defined, xviii, 1
　euangelizomai referring to, xixn22
　infused with passional reason and apologetic content, 66
　overcoming obstacles to faith, xv–xvi
　receiving mixed responses, 12
events, trusting in the Bible, 59
evidence
　allowing the Bible to stand up under scrutiny in a court of law, 59
　cumulative implications of, xx
　making the case and an appeal based on, 42
evil, examples of, 46
existence of God. *See* God's existence
Existential Reasons for Belief in God: A Defense of Desires and Emotions for Faith (Williams), 29
expectation, of hearers putting into practice what they are taught, 22
exploration, other areas of further, 62–65
eyewitness testimony, Paul appealing to, 55

faith
　abduction building a case for, 43
　addressing common objections to, xv
　apologetic preaching as discipleship addressing doubts and providing answers, 14
　apologetics explaining, xxi
　cumulative presentation best in regard to, 36
　defense of, 20
　depending upon the resurrection, 54
　formation of, xvn14
　instructing believers in shared, 19
　involving evidence and certainty, 53
　John's strengthened by his pastor's messages, 65
　making the cumulative abductive case for, 37
　negative apologetics producing answers to challenges, 44
　overcoming obstacles to, xv–xvi
　quoting an opponent of, 45
　reasons to believe, 48–49
　salvation by grace through, xxi
　satisfying needs, 30
　strengthening a disciple's, x
Faith and Reason (Nash), xixn24
false teachers, 16, 20, 21
farewell address, Joshua's second, 37
Father Brown Mysteries (Chesterton), 6
fear, of men regarding the truth of the gospel, 28n8
fiction, presenting the core teachings of Christianity, 6
followers of God, given reasons to remain faithful by Joshua, 40
foreign gods, Paul thought to be a proclaimer of, 9
forgiveness, need for, 30
freedom, 48, 49

Gerhardt, Rick, 3
giving, of early Christians, 4

Index

glorified humanity, retaining a rational-affective capacity, xiiin12
God
  being jealous for the character of, xii
  bringing an end to all evil, 49
  moral nature of, 25–26
  as the source of the Bible, 59
The God Delusion (Dawkins), xiin10
God is Not Great (Hitchens), xiin10
God's existence
  abduction example arguing for, 33–34
  arguing morally relative to, 24
  belief in as a starting point for proclamation, 10
  Craig's version of the cosmological argument for, 35–36
  deductive argument for, 32
  existential argument for, 29–30
  inductive argument for, 32
  making an argument for, xix
  sense of morality as a clue about, ix
"Good News concerning Jesus," preaching centered on, xixn22
goodness, delighting in, 30
gospel
  applying to a particular concern/cultural narrative, 3
  Paul's segue to, 11–12
  as the power of God to salvation, 3
  preaching regarding moral facts, 27
gospel invitation, 12n18, 49–51, 57–58. *See also* invitation
gospel message, resurrection of Jesus as an essential part of, 54

The Great Divorce (Lewis), 6
greatness and goodness, of God under attack, xii
Groothuis, Douglas, 31, 36

Habermas, Gary, 13n1, 14
Harris, Sam, xvi
hastiness, not appropriate in apologetic preaching, 42
Healing, with the gospel as part of COACH, 26n4
Hebrew words, associated with preaching, xviiin20
historic evangelical Christian beliefs, xxn29–xxin20
history, God directing, 11
homiletics training, apologetics and, 63–64
hope, 28, 57
Howard, David M., Jr., 37
Howell, Don N., 16
humanity, morality of, 25–26, 29–30

idol, God as not an, 10
immanence, of God, 11
incarnation, in Jesus Christ, 5
incarnational ministry, example of, 5n9–6n9
induction argument, 32
induction in logical discourse, xx
inductive argumentation, as similar to abductive argumentation, 33
invitation. *See also* gospel invitation
  of Joshua, 41–42
  transition to a related, 52
  transitioning to from the apologetic topic, 59
  used by Paul in Acts, 12n18
Israel, times of disobedience and failure, 40

Index

Jesus Christ. *See also* resurrection of Jesus
  incarnation in, 5
  preaching of, 6
  as the victim of moral evil, 50
Jews, as the primary audience in the early church, 5
John (case study), ix–x, 65
Joshua
  apologetic argument of, 40–41
  concern of, 39–40, 43
  invitation of, 41–42
Joshua 24:1–25, abductive apologetic preaching in, 37–42
Judas, reconciling accounts of his death, 51–52
Jude
  apologetic arguments of, 20–21
  apologetic preaching as discipleship in, 17–23
  epistle of, 18–19
Justin Martyr, xvn15

Kalam Cosmological Argument, Craig's version of, 36n10
Keller, Timothy, 2, 3

Letters to a Christian Nation (Harris), xiin10
Lewis, C. S., 6
life, 11, 30
logical argumentation, Bible and, 63

manipulation, in apologetic preaching, 42
Markos, Louis, 5
Master of Theology, not including apologetics, 64
McDill, Wayne, x–xi
meaning, need for, 30
mechanics of apologetics, 63
mediums, utilizing multiple to communicate, 5–6
metanarrative, reaching postmodern audiences, 6n10
ministerial formation, gap in regard to apologetics and preaching, 64
ministry abilities, adding overall depth to the pastor's, xvii
ministry training academy, author's role in, xivn13
model. *See* STEPS model
moral apologetics
  in apologetic preaching, xxii
  defined, xix–xx, 24
  engaging the whole person, 29
  nuances within, 24n1
  special relationship with preaching, 24–30
moral arguments, 24, 24n1
moral aspect, of Jude's concern, 20
moral center, of the gospel, 26
moral component
  to the gospel, 29
  to Pascal's thought of the gospel, 28n8
moral elements, of Williams' argument for the existence of God, 30
moral evil, examples of, 46
moral facts, 25, 26
moral goodness and knowledge, 25n3, 26
moral laws, requiring a moral lawgiver, 48
moral nature, of God and humanity, 25–26
moral needs, of humans, 29–30
moral obligations, 25–26
moral providence, 25n3, 27
moral savior, need of a perfect, 26
moral transformation, 25n3, 27
moralism, as a means to salvation, 27
morality, innate sense of as clue to God's existence, ix

The Morals of the Story (Baggett and Baggett), 25n3
multi-pastor churches, instances of, xi

natural evil, examples of, 46
natural theology, Paul's use of, 10–11
natural world, 49
needy, sharing with, 4n6
negative apologetics, xix, xixn24, 44, 45–52
negative STEPS model, summarized, 60
Nelson, Richard D., 42
New Atheists, xvi, xvin17
new gods, Socrates accused of introducing, 11n16
new heavens and new earth, xiiin12
A New Kind of Christian (McLaren), xivn13
New Testament, references to preaching, xviiin20
nexus, defined, xn2
now-and-not-yet sense, of apologetic preaching as discipleship, 22–23

obedience, promises of to God, 42
obstacles, removing to Christian growth, 14–17
obstacles to faith, overcoming in evangelistic preaching, xv–xvi
Old Testament
  ideal of community equality, 4n6
  Jude's references to, 20–21
  references to preaching, xviiin20
opponent of Christianity, summarizing the view of, 46–47

Orienting, to the need to the Word of God as part of COACH, 26n4
origin of all peoples/nations, God as, 11
oughtness, 25n3
outline form, of a STEPS example, 51–52, 58–59
oversimplification, 35–37, 47

paradox, of Joshua, 42
Parsons, Mikeal C., 11
Pascal, Blaise, 28n8
passional reason, engaging, 27–30
pastoral counsel, apologetics and, xvii
pastoral direction, of Jude, 21
pastoral ministry, types of young men entering, xiv
pastors. *See also* preachers
  adding depth to ministry abilities, xvii
  apologetic engagement in preaching, xiii
  having little knowledge of apologetics, xii
  role as preachers, xi
  serving the counseling process, 64
Paul
  admonition to "preach the word!" 66
  message to philosophers and others on Mars Hill in Athens, 7–8
  motivation for his message on Mars Hill, 8–9
  on preaching, xi
  segue to the gospel and appeal to the audience, 11–12
  sharing the gospel on Mars Hill, 37
  testifying on the resurrection, 55

Index

use of common ground, 9–10
use of natural theology and cultural elements, 10–11
willingness to become all things to all men for the gospel's sake, 5n9–6n9
personhood, innate moral aspects of, 29
Peter, 28, 29
Pharisee, Paul as a former, 9n13
plausibility, not confusing with credibility, 36
pluralism, veneration of philosophical and religious, xi
poetry (culture), providing a reference to God, 11
positive apologetics, xix, xixn24, 44–45, 52–53
positive case for believing, 53
positive STEPS model, summarized, 60
post moderns, yearning to break out of the box, 5
post-Christian world, incredulous that anyone would think like a Christian, xii
practical applications
  transitioning from apologetic case-making to, 56
  truth of any worldview logically linked to, 3
The Preacher and His Models (Stalker), xixn23
preachers. *See also* pastors
  avoiding the language of doubt, 53
  believing in the value of apologetics, xiv
  communicating the gospel in a relevant manner, 6
  softening hard truths in the Bible, xiv
  teaching the "how" of apologetics, 15–16
preaching. *See also* apologetic preaching; evangelistic preaching
  answering questions about God, ix
  apologetics and, xv–xvii, 65
  defined, xviii, xviiin21
  described, x
  to disciples, xixn23
  goal of, xviiin21
  in a post-everything context, x–xiii
  role of moral apologetics within, 24–30
  from the theoretical perspective, 63
preaching as discipleship, defined, xix, 13
preaching as evangelism, defined, xviii
premises
  in a deductive argument, xx, 32
  in an induction argument, xx
Preparing Evangelistic Sermons (Richard), xviiin22–xixn22
proclamation, of God's message, xviii

rational moral elements, 30
real life needs, making apologetic realities fit, 56
reasons, 48–49, 53
relevance, 5
responses
  by Paul's hearers, 12
  to sermons, 12
resurrection of Jesus. *See also* Jesus Christ
  argument in favor of belief, 55–56
  attempts to disprove, xv–xvi
  beginning a positive apoogetic message on, 53
  biblical evidence for, 54, 55–56

resurrection of Jesus *(continued)*
  bringing power through the Spirit, 56
  detractors from, xvi
  as the final hope for an end to suffering, 57
  as an invitation, 57–58
  Paul's message ending with a proclamation of, 12
  practical application of, 56–57
Robinson, Haddon W., xi

salvation, by grace through faith, xxi
sarcasm, avoiding, 47
Savior, trusting, 59
Scripture
  faithfulness to, 65
  reliability of, 51, 58–59
seeker or skeptic, 2, 3
seekers, xiv, 1–12
selfcare, of believers, 22
seminary, not including any training in apologetics, 64
sensus divinitatis, found within all persons, 29
sermon structure, in discipleship preaching, 26n4
sermons, value of apologetic content in, xiv–xv
Sheila (case study example), ix, 65
significance, in positive apologetics, 53–54
sin, humanity's problem with, 26
Sire, James W., 2
skeptics, xii, xiv
skeptics and seekers, x
Smither, Edward L., 15
"so what" question, 7n11, 61–62
Socrates, 11n16
source of all life, God as, 10
sources, of doubt, 14
sovereignty, of God, 10

Stalker, James, on preaching to disciples, xixn23
STEPS model
  for apologetic preaching, 44–60, 62
  moving from the possible to the actual, xxii
  for negative apologetics in outline form, 51–52
  negative summarized, 60
  for positive apologetics, 52–59, 60
striving with great intensity, apologetic task of, 20
suzerainty treaties, between a lord and a vassal, 40

Taylor, Douglas E., 17
tentmaker, Paul as, 9n13
theological aspect, of Jude's concern, 20
theses, regarding preaching and apologetics, 65
Timothy, as a pastor and mentor, xi
TO THE UNKNOWN GOD, inscription noted by Paul, 9
transition, in a positive apologetic message, 57
truth
  of Christianity, 35
  speaking in love, 22

unbeliever's worldview, engaging, 2–3

Wainwright, William J., 28
Watson, Duane F., 21n16
weaknesses, presenting in a critic's argument, 47–48
White, James E., xi
Williams, Clifford, 29–30
winning a soul, 2

word and deed, example of the power of, 5n7
word-and-deed approach, employing, 3–5
worldview
    Christian, x, 2, 36
    credibility of, 36
    engaging an unbeliever's, 2–3
Wytsma, Ken, 3

www.ingramcontent.com/pod-product-compliance
Lightning Source LLC
Chambersburg PA
CBHW070514090426
42735CB00012B/2774